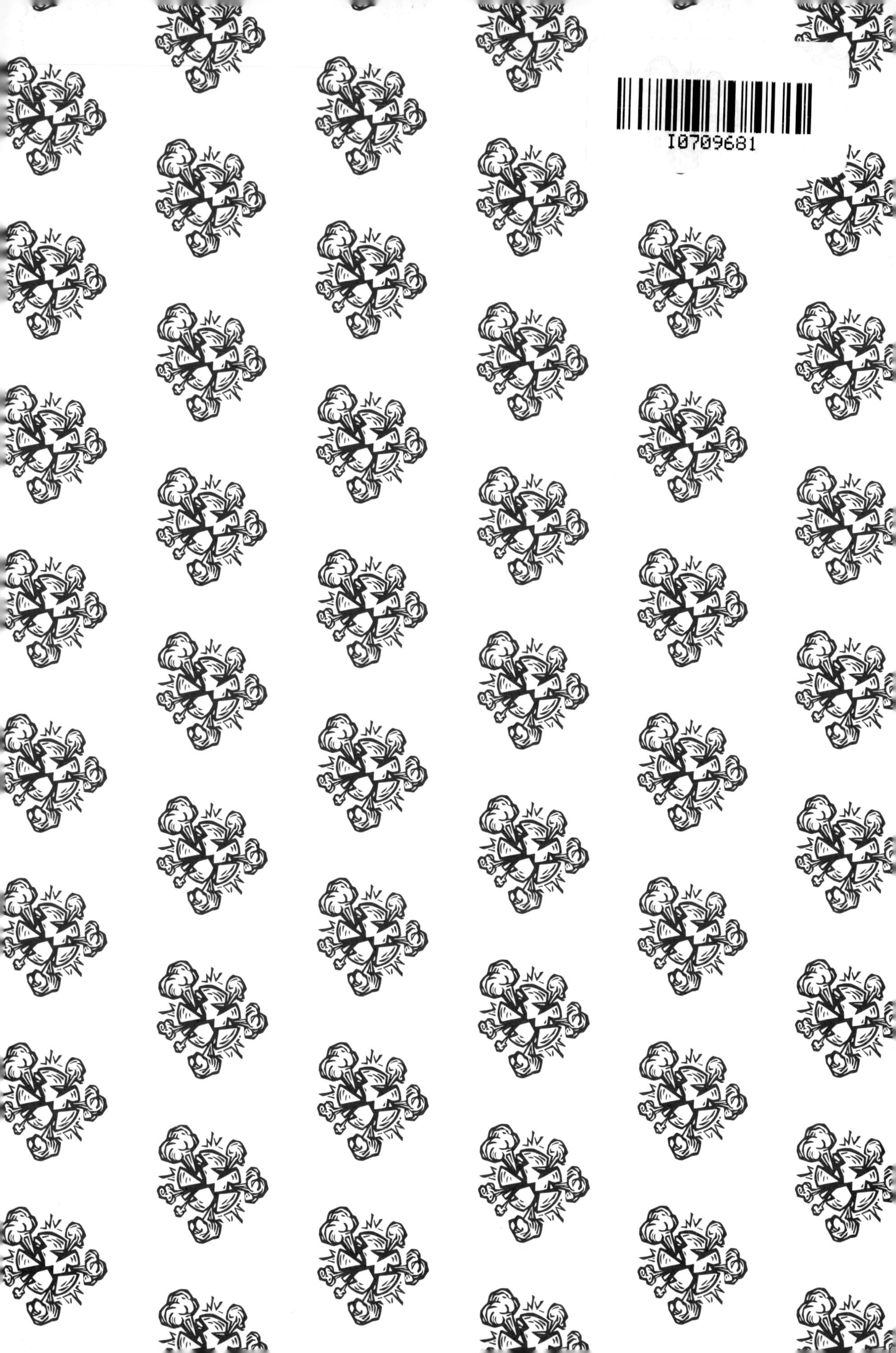

The END Is At HAND

An Illustrated History of the Apocalypse

Darrel Perkins

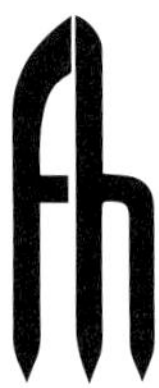

*"The optimist invents the plane,
the pessimist invents the parachute."*

George Bernard Shaw

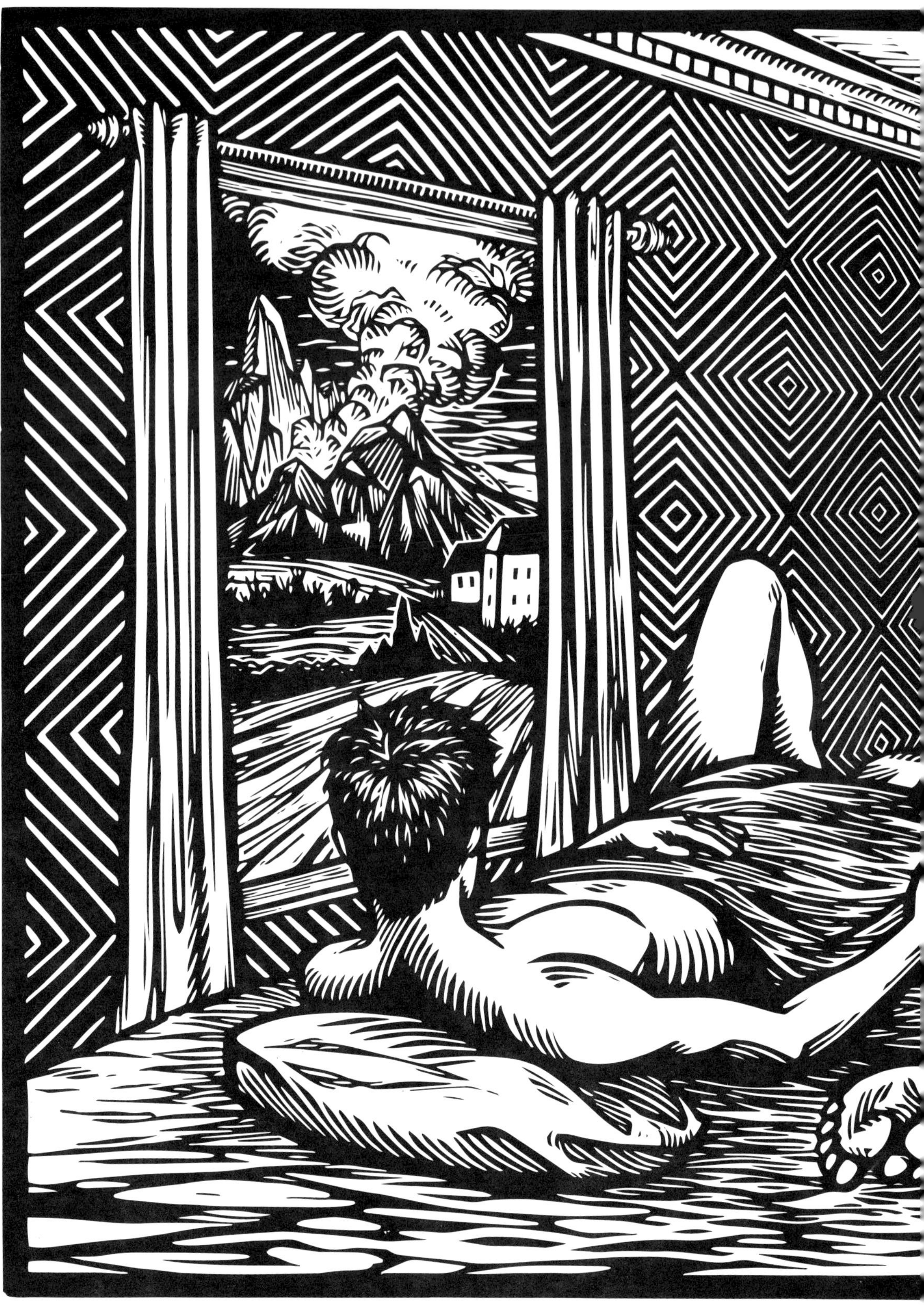

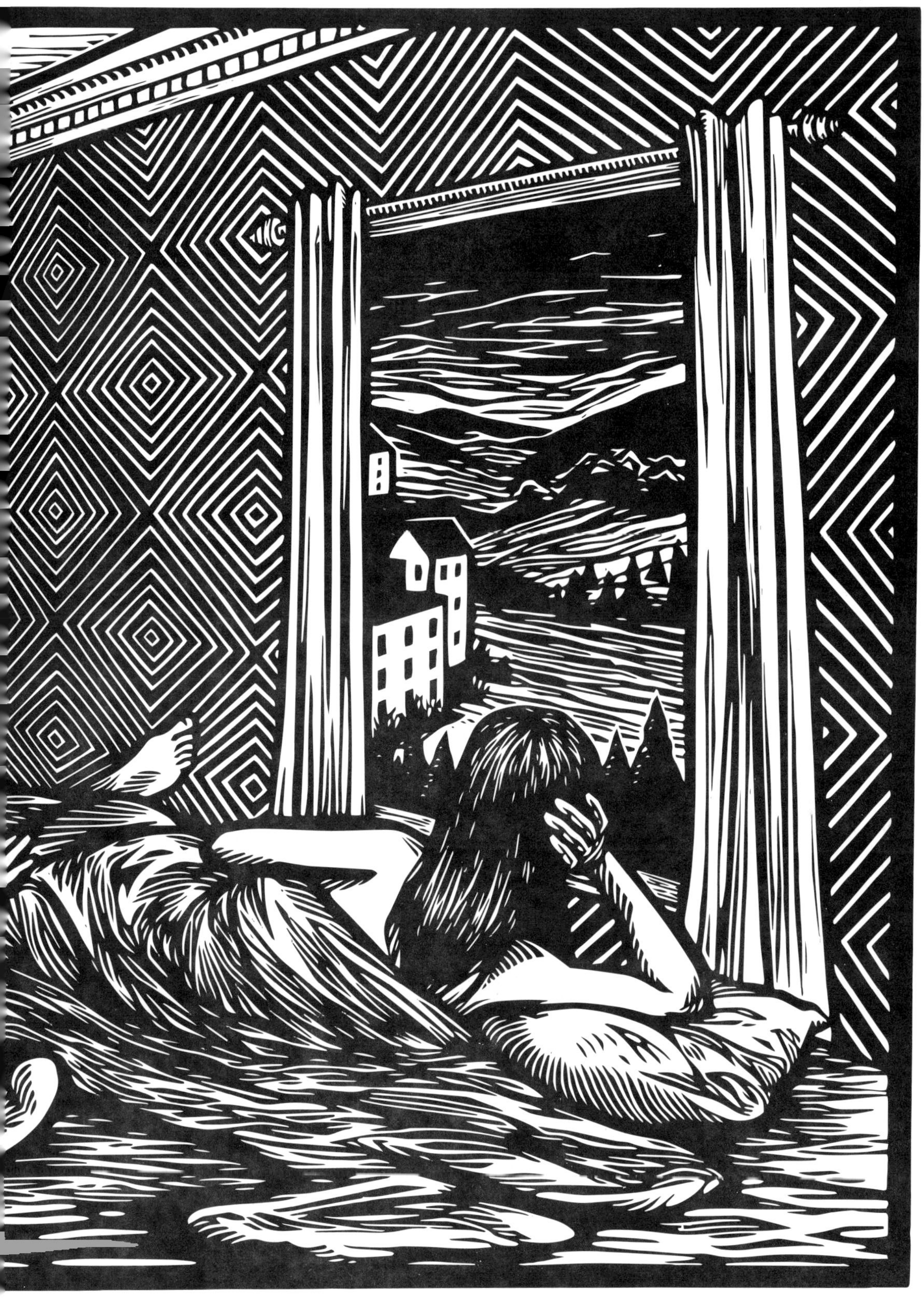

Contents

Introduction

No one wants to be the middle child of history. If the world were to end in our lifetime, we would become a part of something bigger than ourselves. The most significant event imaginable is more exciting than the thought of being just another organism passing along an infinite timeline. Putting aside whatever immediate agony the apocalypse may bring, the long-term reward is the gift of eternal bragging rights in the afterlife. You had to be there.

The End has been debated since the Beginning. We may not always agree on how the world will end, but we're full of ideas. When we think we have the answer, we naturally want to share our discovery with everyone. A pessimistic outlook could save the world, if we're right. So we take to the streets, or more recently the internet, with picket signs to shout the news: THE END IS AT HAND. Parts of the message might even be justifiable, since the world has no shortage of neglected issues that could use our attention. Most of us dismiss these alarms, and for good reason. Unfortunately, it's hard to tell the difference between genuine risk and genuine crazy.

Full of confusion and misdirected concerns, our outrage often turns to wasted hysteria. When it's suggested that everything we know could be gone in an instant, we get emotional. Those strong feelings can be easily manipulated. The End has historically attracted swindlers looking to gain power or money. Any time a speaker uses fear to motivate a crowd, it's worth questioning what they have to gain from our vulnerability. Will the message improve the world or is it rooted in self-interest? What are we actually mad about?

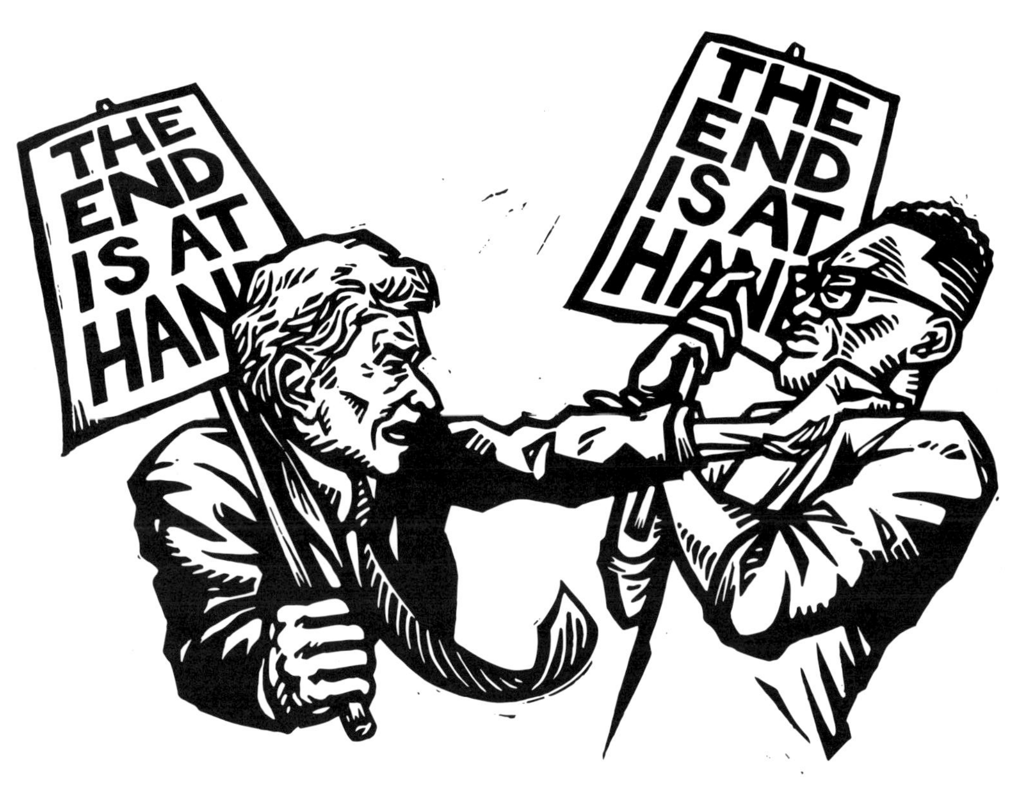

THE
END
IS AT
HAN
THE
END
IS AT
HAN

These stories examine how the world has ended before, when we mistakenly thought it would end again, and how it could end in the future. When communities experience hardship, they develop myths to explain the past and instill a sense of security about the future. Unavoidable disasters require stories that give purpose to the otherwise senseless loss. Avoidable disasters force us to reflect upon our own impact on the world around us. When we think about the fate of the world, we're really responding to the state of the world today.

We exist in multiple worlds at once, and we have questions about how all of them will end. A society is only three missed meals from collapse, the planet is only two degrees from climate catastrophe, and the universe is... well, we don't know yet. All of these old faithful structures will someday be gone, which can be both liberating and tragic to think about. One way to cope is by finding reason in how and why our worlds will cease to be. Believing in destiny can help people feel like there is a greater plan beyond our control. It's one less thing to worry about.

Every generation has their own hardship that no one else can understand. Talk to a survivor of war, famine, or plague and they may admit to thinking the End was near at some point. Thankfully, we're more resilient than we give ourselves credit for. Our way of living may change drastically throughout a lifetime, but perspective is important. Change is the only constant in existence, and an ending is just another form of change. We should come to expect it, even when any disturbance to our normal life feels like the end of the world. The Earth endures volcanos, asteroids, and atomic bombs. It adapts and survives; we can do the same.

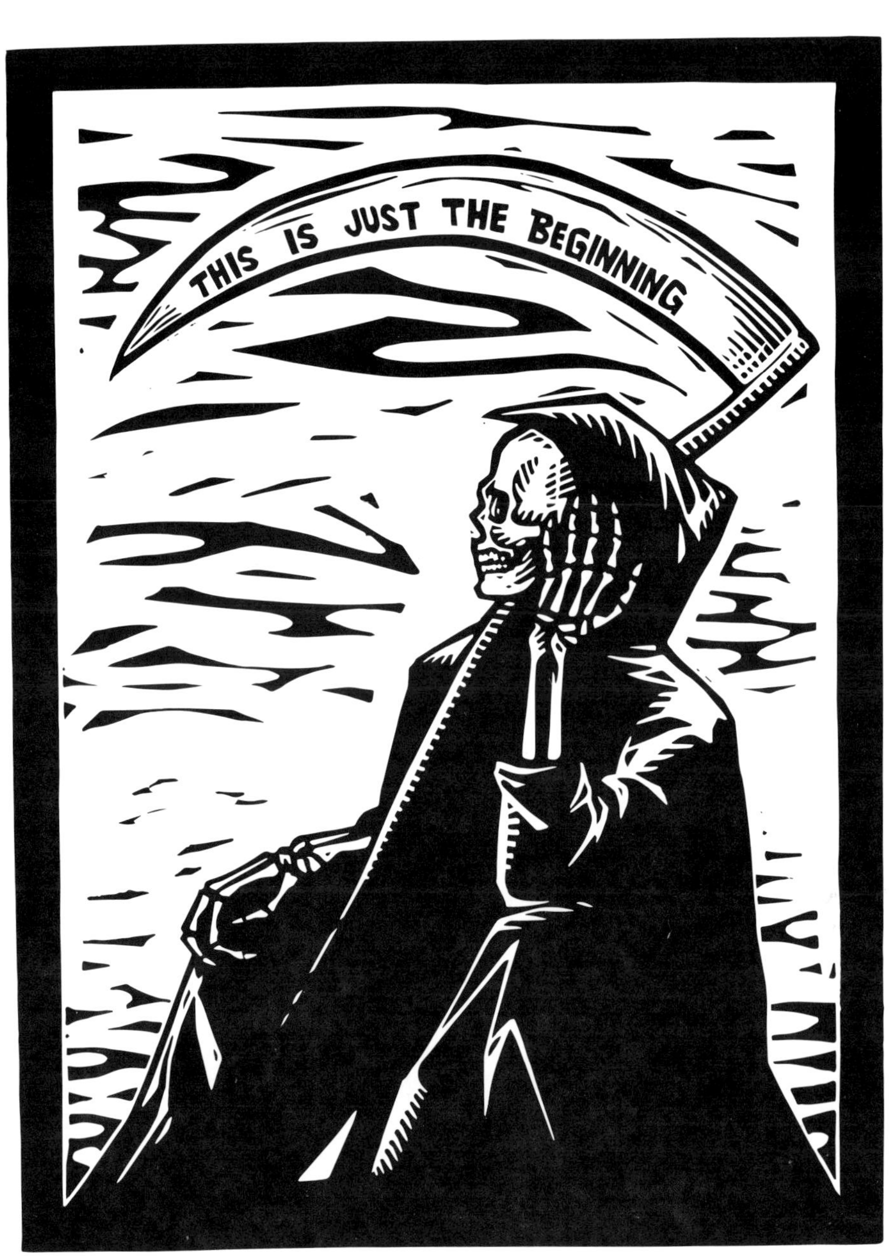
THIS IS JUST THE BEGINNING

Mass Extinction

Let the dodo be a warning to us all. The flightless bird inhabited an island without predators, so they fearlessly approached hungry sailors that arrived in the 1600s. Before long, there were no dodos to be found. One day there was tasty tropical fowl aplenty, and the next they were gone. It was around this time that the idea of "extinction" was proposed. Previously, any unidentifiable bones were assumed to be from species that still existed but migrated elsewhere, or from mythical creatures like dragons and unicorns that were too rare to be seen. It was a shocking realization that a species could be hunted until it disappears *forever*. We are now coming to a realization that, like the dodo, our shortsighted actions may be causing our own demise.

Over 99 percent of species that have ever lived are already extinct. Some of these disappearances happen gradually, but there have been five catastrophes on Earth resulting in mass extinction. The causes were global cooling, fluctuating oxygen levels caused by algae growth, two volcanic eruptions, then an asteroid collision. We might currently be in the beginning of the planet's sixth mass extinction, this time due to a loss of biodiversity. Like anyone stuck in a dead-end existence, our ecosystem is missing that lush variety that makes life grand. Species are disappearing hundreds of times faster than they would naturally, with up to a million types of plants and animals in danger. The major contributing factors are deforestation, pollution, overconsumption of meat and fish, and the spread of invasive species. Strict guidelines for global nature conservation would be a safe option to secure life for future generations. Alternatively, we could preserve our existence in a museum next to the dodo and a description of what flowers used to smell like.

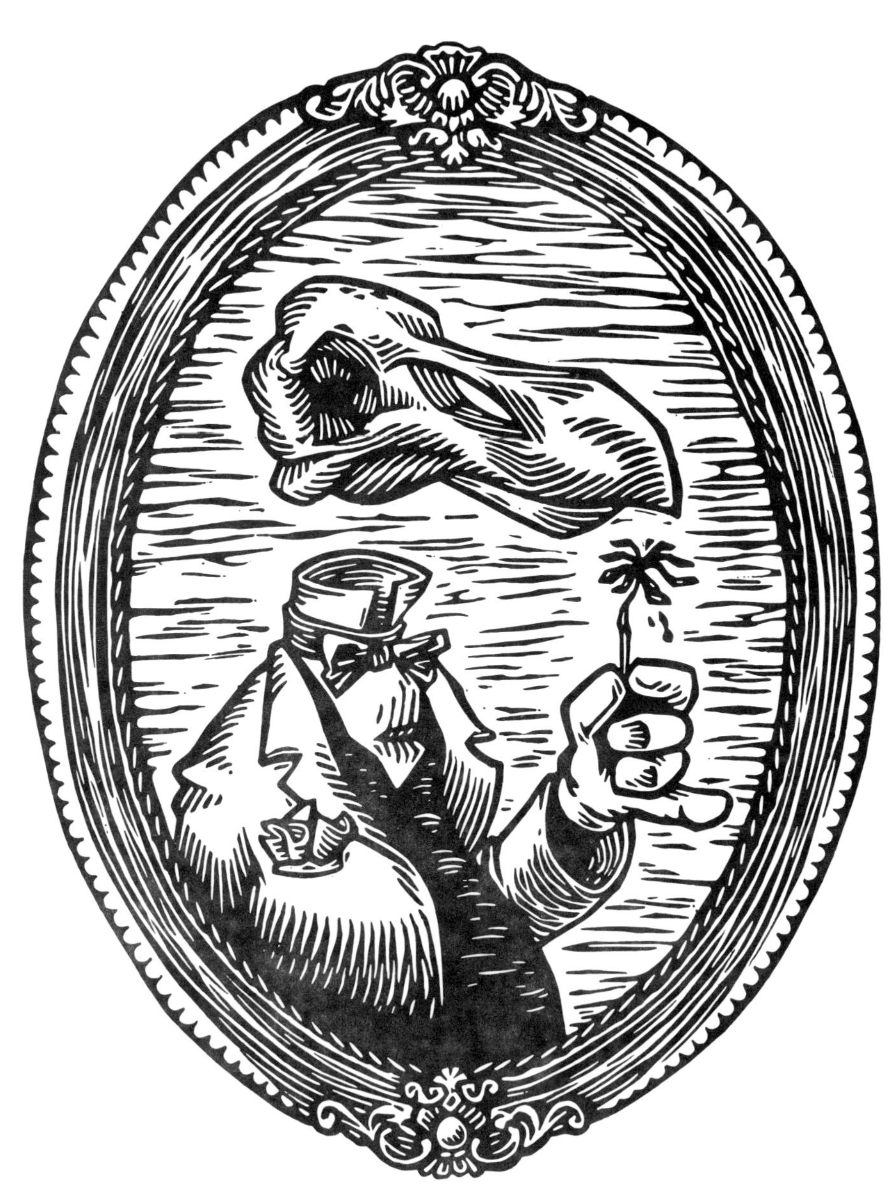

Volcanos

A volcano erupts about every week on Earth, to varying degrees of destruction. These neon-red and smoky phenomena have the ability to wipe out life as we know it, which is exactly what happened about 250 million years ago. Known as the Great Dying, a massive amount of lava spewed from a volcano located in what is now Siberia, triggering the release of greenhouse gases that disrupted ecosystems across the globe. About 96 percent of marine species and three-quarters of species on land died out. It was a major reset of the planet's trajectory.

Life eventually returned, then was wiped out by another supervolcano fifty million years later, bringing the Triassic period to a halt. By the time humans arrive, they inherit a pronounced fear of the volcano. Myths are shared by tribes and passed down for generations—a ritual that helps people cope with disaster and the unknown.

Volcanos are considered one of the most likely ways the world could end. By historical average, we're overdue for an eruption from one of Earth's twenty supervolcanos. This very bad day would begin with increasingly intense earthquakes as magma forces its way to the surface. Lava explodes violently into the air, lighting the sky ablaze. Vast expanses of land would be covered in toxic ash made of splintered rock and glass. Giant clouds smother the Earth and block sunlight, forcing global temperatures to plummet. Agriculture and rainforests are annihilated. It would be several years before life stabilizes.

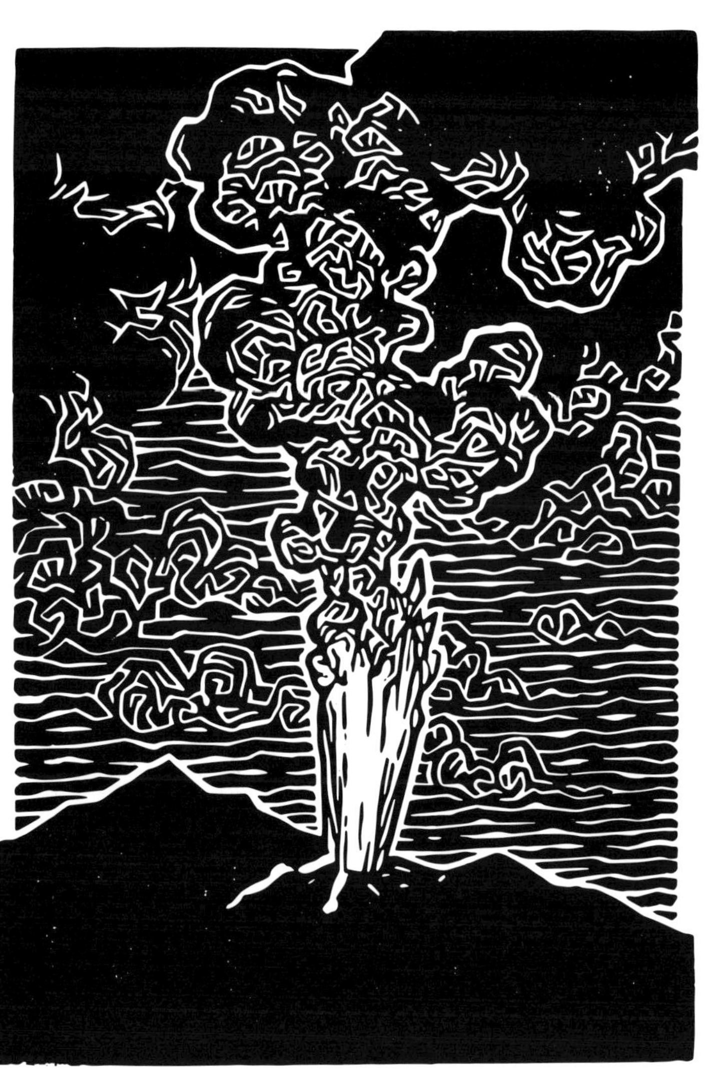

Astronomical Impact

Much of Earth's history has been shaped by collisions between astronomical objects. Long before becoming the proud home of all life in our solar system, an early molten Earth likely collided with another small planet, leaving rubble to amass in our orbit and form the moon. That dusty old attic in the sky now gives us lunar tides and monthly calendars. Astronomical impact may also be credited with our oceans, which possibly arrived by icy rocks landing on the young planet. Earth still receives a constant sprinkling of space dust, but life-altering impacts only happen about every twenty million years.

Sixty-six million years ago, a giant asteroid hit the waters off what is now Mexico. It ignited wildfires on land, sent a huge tsunami rippling across the globe, and spewed debris high into the atmosphere. Severe global cooling wiped out three-quarters of life on Earth, making it our most recent mass extinction. It killed off most dinosaurs, but the survivors became ancestors of many reptile and bird species of today. Evolution doesn't end, but it does take detours.

Could it happen again? It's a matter of *when* Earth will be hit with another devastating asteroid, not *if*. Stephen Hawking estimated an asteroid collision to be the biggest threat to the planet. NASA has warned that scientists are unprepared and would need five years to develop defensive measures. One proposal to avoid impact is to deflect the asteroid into an altered path away from Earth. Another would be to fragment the asteroid into smaller particles that could burn up in Earth's atmosphere. These promising solutions are becoming more possible thanks to technological advances. We may be overdue for a major astronomical impact, but humans now appear to have a better chance of survival than our dinosaur predecessors.

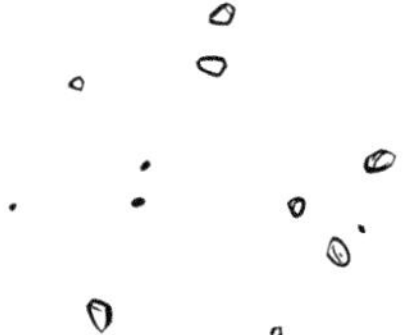

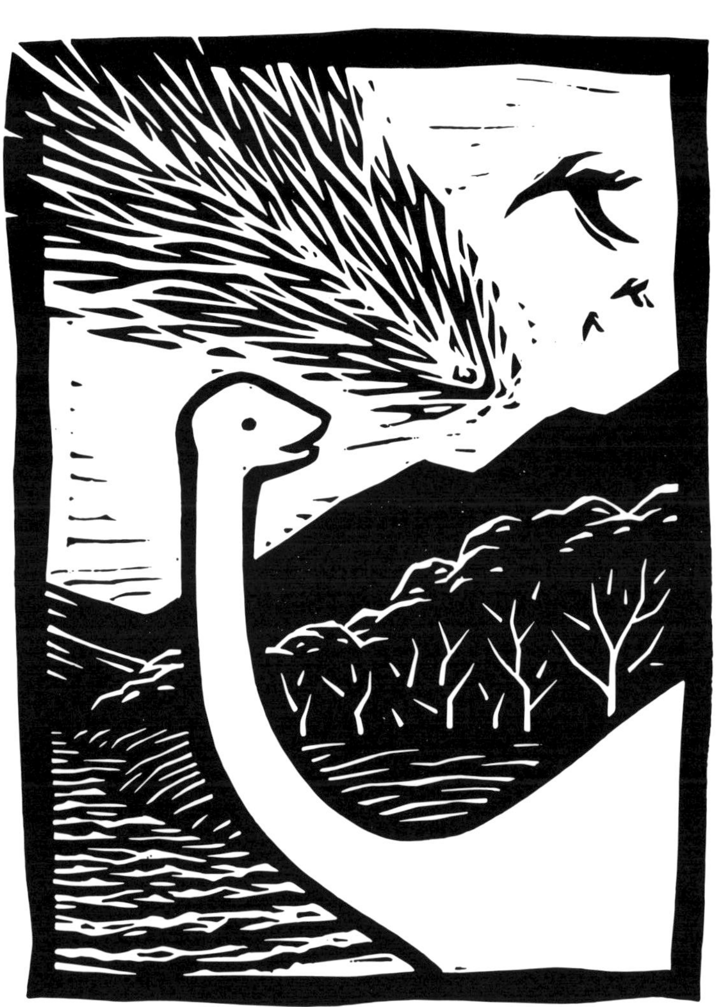

Eschatology

About 11,000 years ago, humans began to move beyond a hunter-gatherer lifestyle by developing reliable agriculture. This new comfort gave people time to ponder the world around them. Eschatology is how religions answer our existential questions about finality, including immortality of the soul, rebirth, resurrection, and the end of the world.

The Hindu believe that our current life cycle will end when the world is overrun with evil, then reborn in a new age of innocence.

According to Judaism, the end of days will occur when Jewish people return to Israel, the King Messiah appears, and God resurrects the dead.

Buddhists predict that after the degeneration of humanity, the world will enter a new era in which the next Buddha will appear.

The Christian Bible states that the end times will be marked by widespread disaster and war, the Second Coming of Jesus Christ, and concluding with virtuous people being raptured and lifted directly into Heaven.

In Islam, the Quran says that after the annihilation of all life on Earth, Allah will resurrect the dead and pass a final judgment to eternally separate the righteous and the wicked.

Rastafarians believe Selassie, God incarnate, will arrive for the day of judgment and return home those taken from Africa through the slave trade, bringing an era of world peace.

These religions originated in different times and places but share similar outcomes for the world. Recurring themes feature the world falling apart, existence of an afterlife or cycle, and redemption for those that led honorable lives.

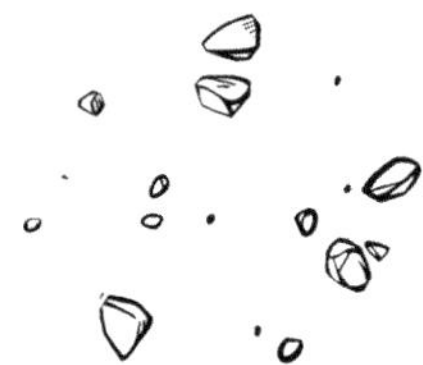

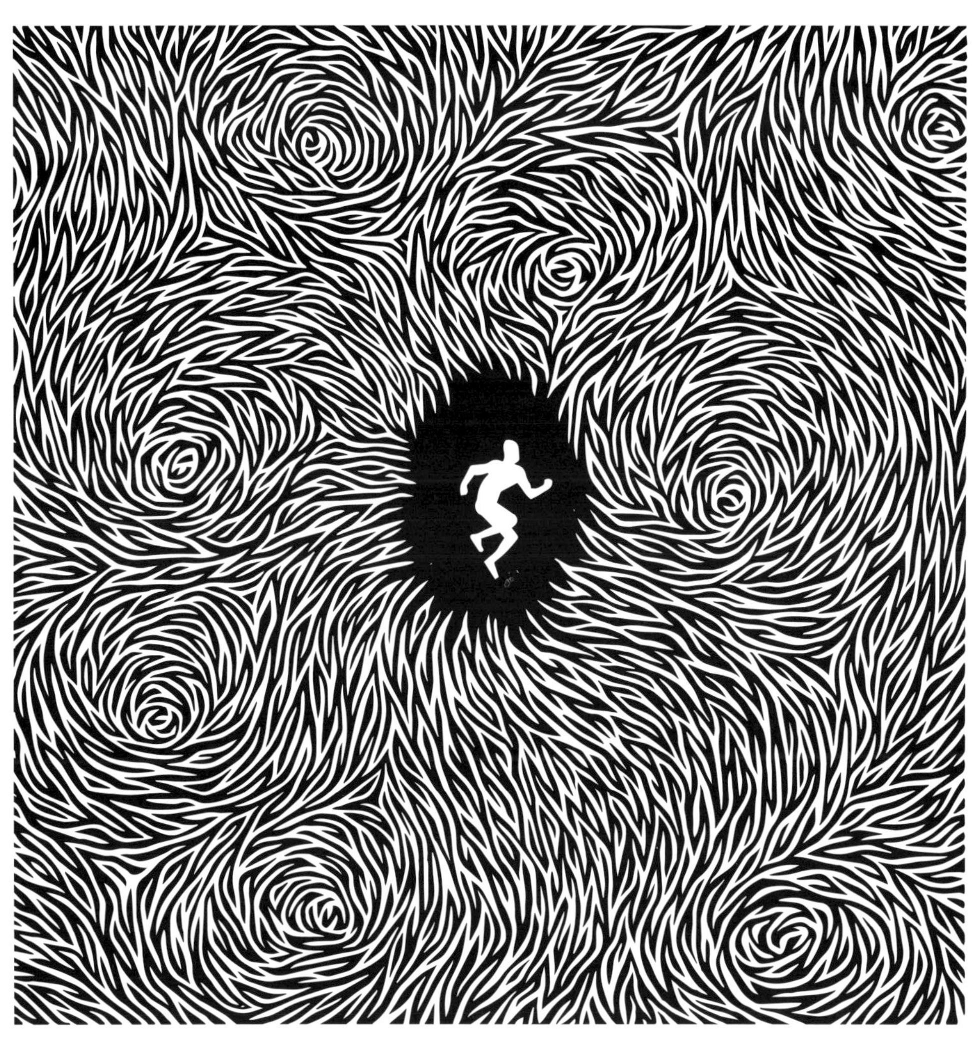

Noah's Ark

The story of Noah's Ark is one of the most frequently shared tales of apocalypse in history. It begins with an extraordinary man named Noah receiving a request from God to construct a massive wooden boat. Noah builds the ark and packs it with a male and female pair of every animal species he can find. As they set sail, God sends a scourge of rain to flood the Earth. The deluge drowns the wicked but spares Noah, his family, and the many animals he secured. All of life today is descended from the survivors.

Versions of Noah's Ark have been adopted by Judaism, Christianity, and Islam, but it was a popular folktale before those religions were formed. The earliest documentation dates back to the Sumerians in Mesopotamia about 4,000 years ago. Going back even further, an oral tradition of the story might have begun with extensive flooding of the Tigris and Euphrates rivers about 5,000 years ago. There isn't enough water on the planet for a global flood, but seeing entire cities swept away would lead survivors to think the whole world was affected. People migrated around Europe, Africa, and the Middle East, sharing sensational accounts as they moved.

Noah's story endures partly because it's attached to major religions of the world, but also because of its sympathetic components. It has a righteous hero facing global catastrophe, hard work paying off, and lovable animals. It's an entertaining tragedy for the whole family.

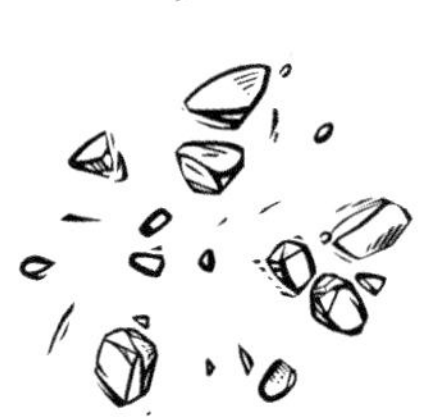

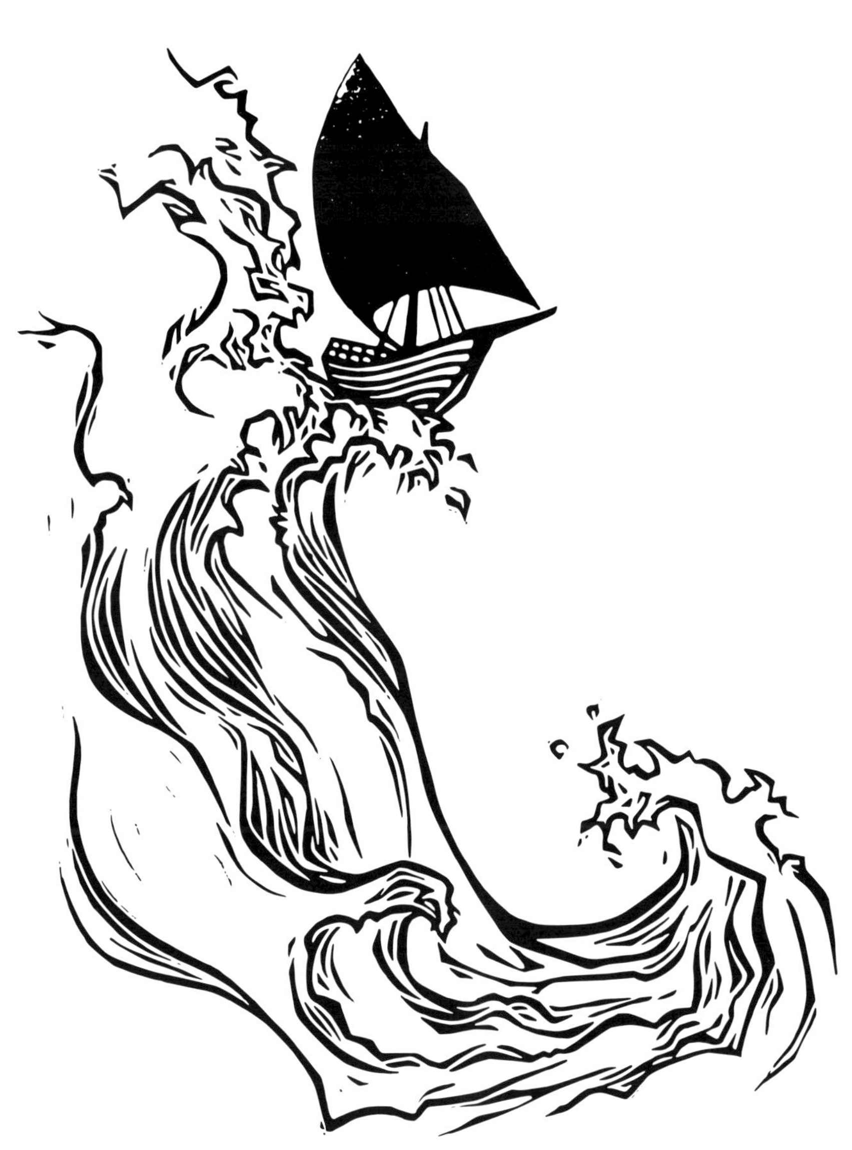

Kalki, the One Who Will End Time

Hinduism is the world's oldest major religion, with customs and stories dating back over 4,000 years. According to Hinduism, the universe is cyclical and will continue through infinite eras of existence. Our present age is predicted to be full of quarrel and strife. So far, this checks out. Despite the many honorable people of the world, their positive impact becomes increasingly negated by a growing dominance of the wicked. Society will continue to deteriorate until absolute evil rules over the few remaining virtuous souls.

With morality on the brink of extinction, Kalki arrives. He is the tenth and final incarnation of Lord Vishnu, the immortal God of protection and sustenance. The name Kalki might be derived from the word *kala*, meaning time, so he is sometimes thought of as "The One Who Will End Time." Riding in from the sky on a white horse, the warrior God swings a sword blazing like a comet. He annihilates all the evil rulers of the world, restoring Earth to its former purity. Once his task is complete, Kalki returns to a deep meditation in the stars, where he awaits patiently for the next call to action.

When we read the dour news of the day, it may seem Kalki is just around the corner, ready to usher in a new and noble world. However, Hindu cycles are long and we still have an estimated 427,000 years of corruption in our current age. Until then, keep looking for white horses in the sky.

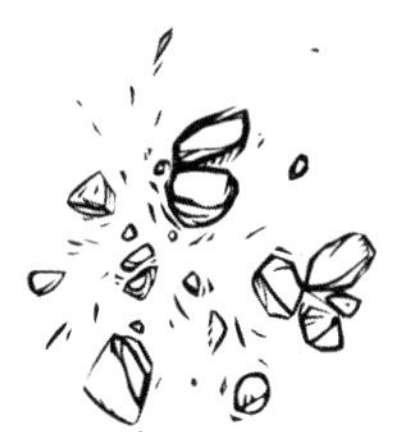

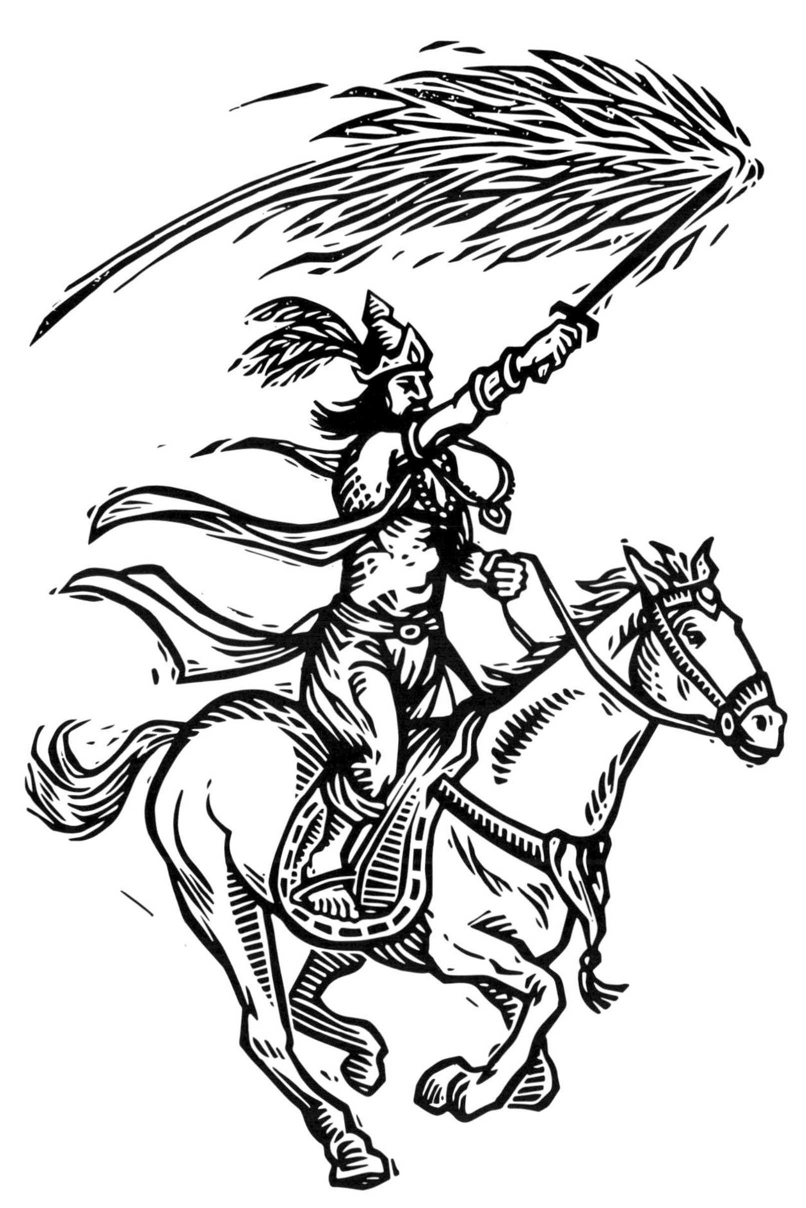

Religious Conflict

The Book of Revelation is the final part of the Bible and it focuses largely on Christian eschatology. It depicts a war in Heaven between angels and the Devil, ending with the Devil falling to Earth and leading the whole world astray.

The passage may be symbolic for the many conflicts between religious communities throughout history. Worshippers embody the heavenly battle between good and evil. The devout view themselves as the angels, while anyone opposed to their God would be a messenger of Satan. This theory credits the Devil with our holy wars of hate including the Christian Crusade against Muslim expansion, the Troubles in Ireland between Protestants and Catholics, and the Israel-Palestine conflict in the Middle East. If the world ends by war in the name of faith, some would interpret it as biblical evidence that the Devil made them do it.

Religion, money, and race are the most common causes of human conflict. They're very distinct parts of the human ordeal, which can be complicated. Most beliefs evolve throughout our lifetime, but a few, like religion, can be so uncompromising that believers would rather die than accept another. Connection to a higher cause can be a powerful motivator, which can bring transcendent peace or tremendous death, depending on how those feelings are directed. Religious doctrines often preach about morality and goodwill, but every major affiliation has had violence committed in its name at some point. The world can either find peace with our diversity of beliefs or continue fighting under the Devil's rule.

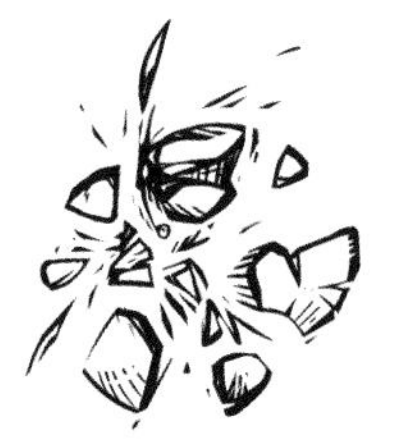

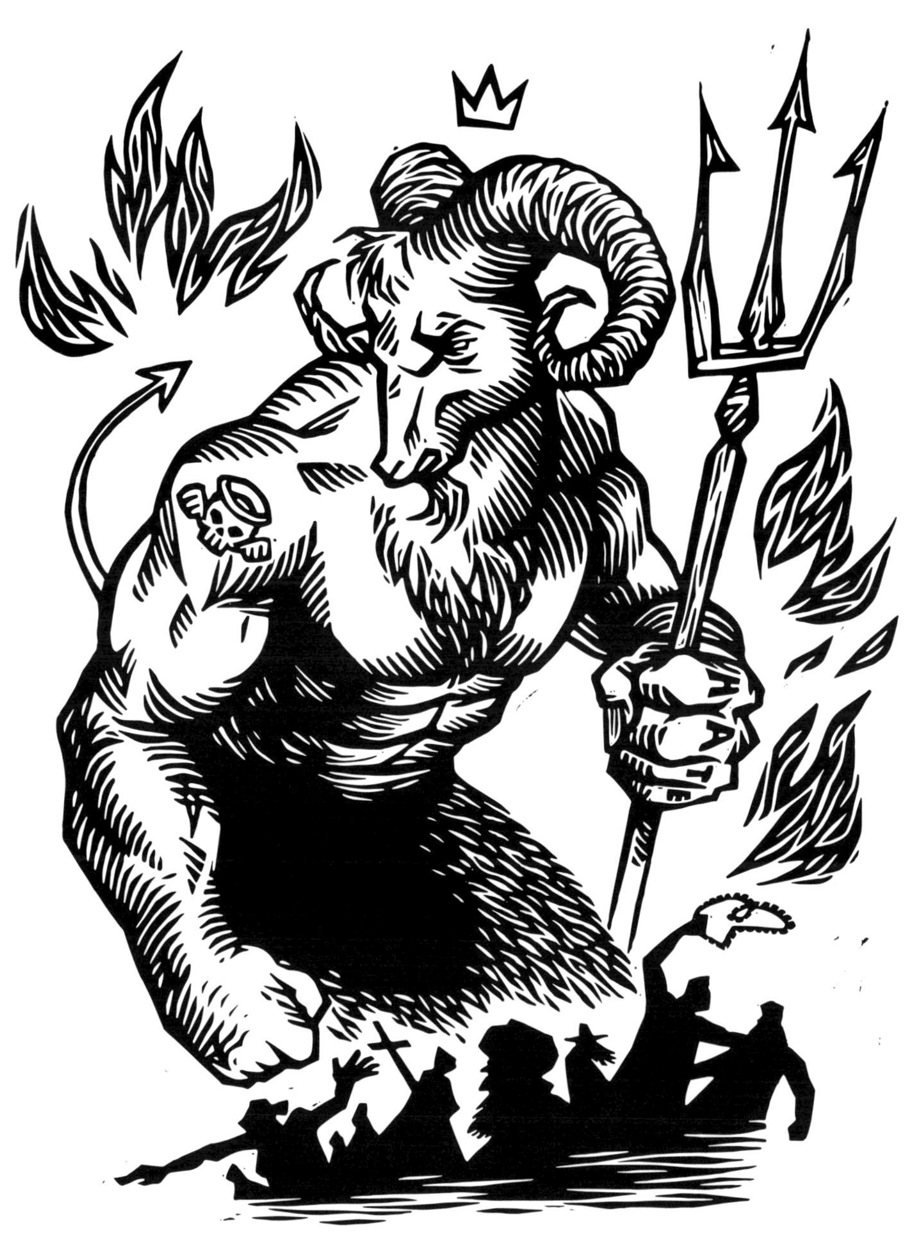

Four Horsemen of the Apocalypse

When the time has come, four beings will arrive on horseback to set in motion the cataclysm of the Christian apocalypse. Each horseman conveys a particular role in destroying the world.

The first horseman delivers *Conquest* with a crown and bow. Riding a white horse, this strong man is intent on dominating the world. History has brought us many despotic leaders that would fit this mold.

The second horseman brings *War* and bloodshed. Riding a red horse and carrying a great sword, he is here to disrupt peace on Earth and compel people to kill each other. Perhaps you've felt this horseman possess you when another car cuts you off in traffic.

The third horseman inflicts *Famine* on the world. On a black horse and balancing a scale, this rider represents the greed in society that creates imbalance in the sharing of essential goods. When you read a news story about a billionaire hoarding their wealth to the detriment of the world, this horseman has arrived.

The fourth horseman rides a sickly horse and brings vast *Death* to the world, often in the form of plague. That will never happen—right?

When these events occur simultaneously, they are often interpreted as a warning that the Last Days are upon us. Despite our best efforts to avoid these conflicts, they tend to happen on a fairly regular basis.

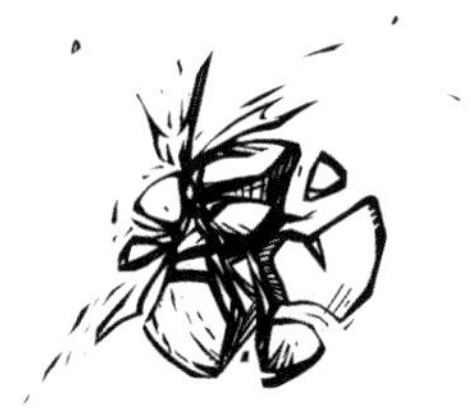

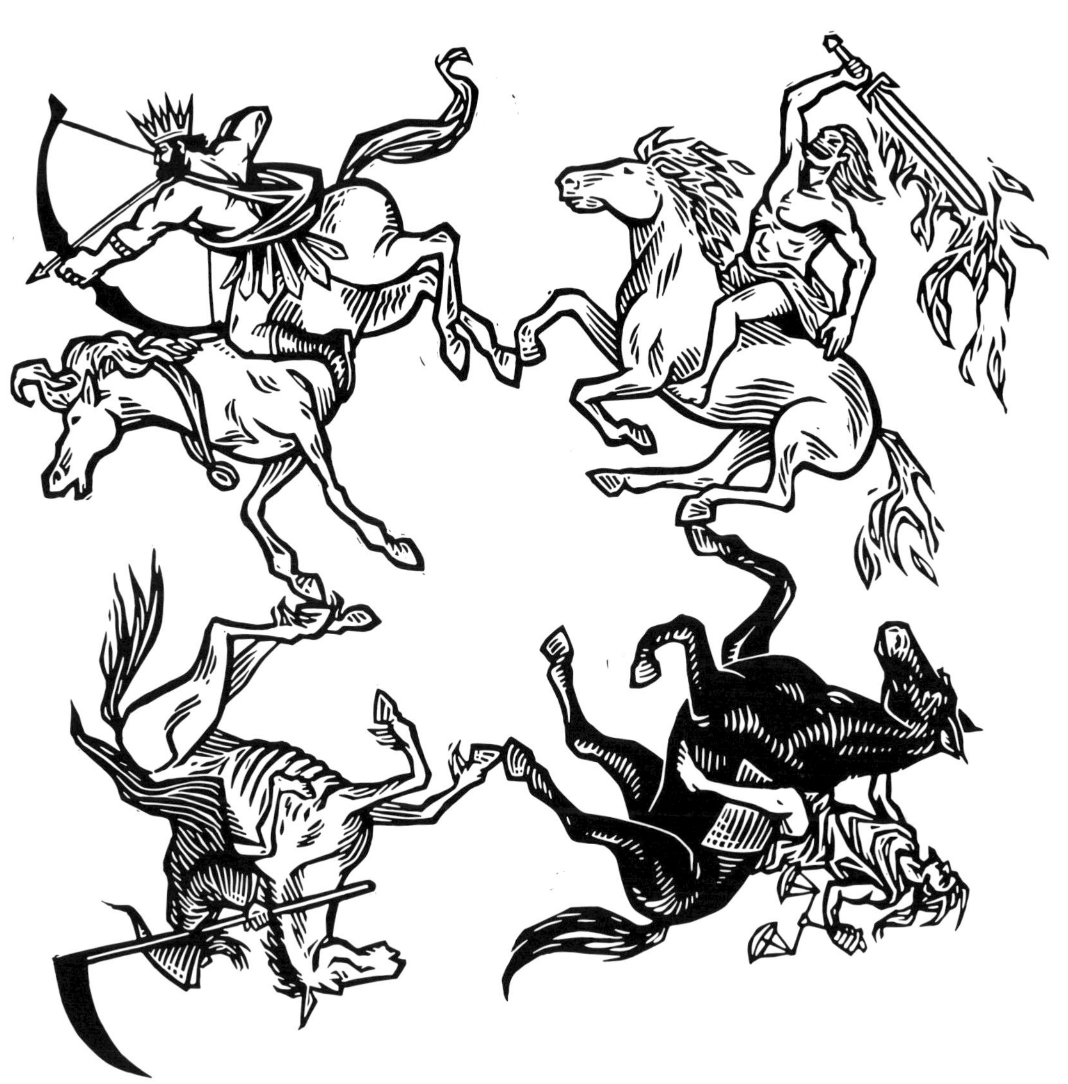

Yajuj and Majuj

In a prophecy from Islamic eschatology,* Yajuj and Majuj are two unholy tribes that once terrorized the lands surrounding the Caucasus Mountains. These barbaric forces came down from the mountains to steal, kill, and generally inflict anarchy on the peaceful lives of nearby villagers.

Victims of Yajuj and Majuj asked righteous king Dhul Qarnayn for help. He built an impenetrable wall between two mountains to block the fiends from the rest of the world, where they stay to this day. The tribes dig and hammer and strike at the barrier every day, but every night Allah repairs it to protect the innocent.

Someday, in a major sign that the end is near, Allah will allow Yajuj and Majuj to emerge from behind the wall. They will surge down the mountains, killing and pillaging their way across the world. Everything in their path will be destroyed, including crops, trees, and entire villages. When the insatiable mobs pass through, the prophecy foretells the tribesmen drinking up a large lake in a single day.

After everyone is dead and the world's resources are decimated, the tribes will grow arrogant with their dominance. They confidently set their attention to the inhabitants of Heaven. Yajuj and Majuj shoot arrows into the sky, which fall from the clouds covered in the blood of Heaven's keepers. When it seems the barbarians are close to conquering Heaven and Earth, a vengeful Allah responds. He sends insects and worms to crawl into their orifices and kill every member of Yajuj and Majuj. Their decaying bodies return to the soil to nourish the renewed Earth and their souls will spend eternity in Hell.

---

* Broad variations of the story exist in Judaism and Christianity, where they're named Gog and Magog.

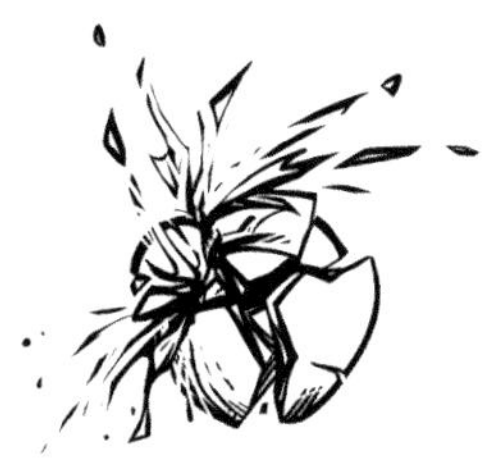

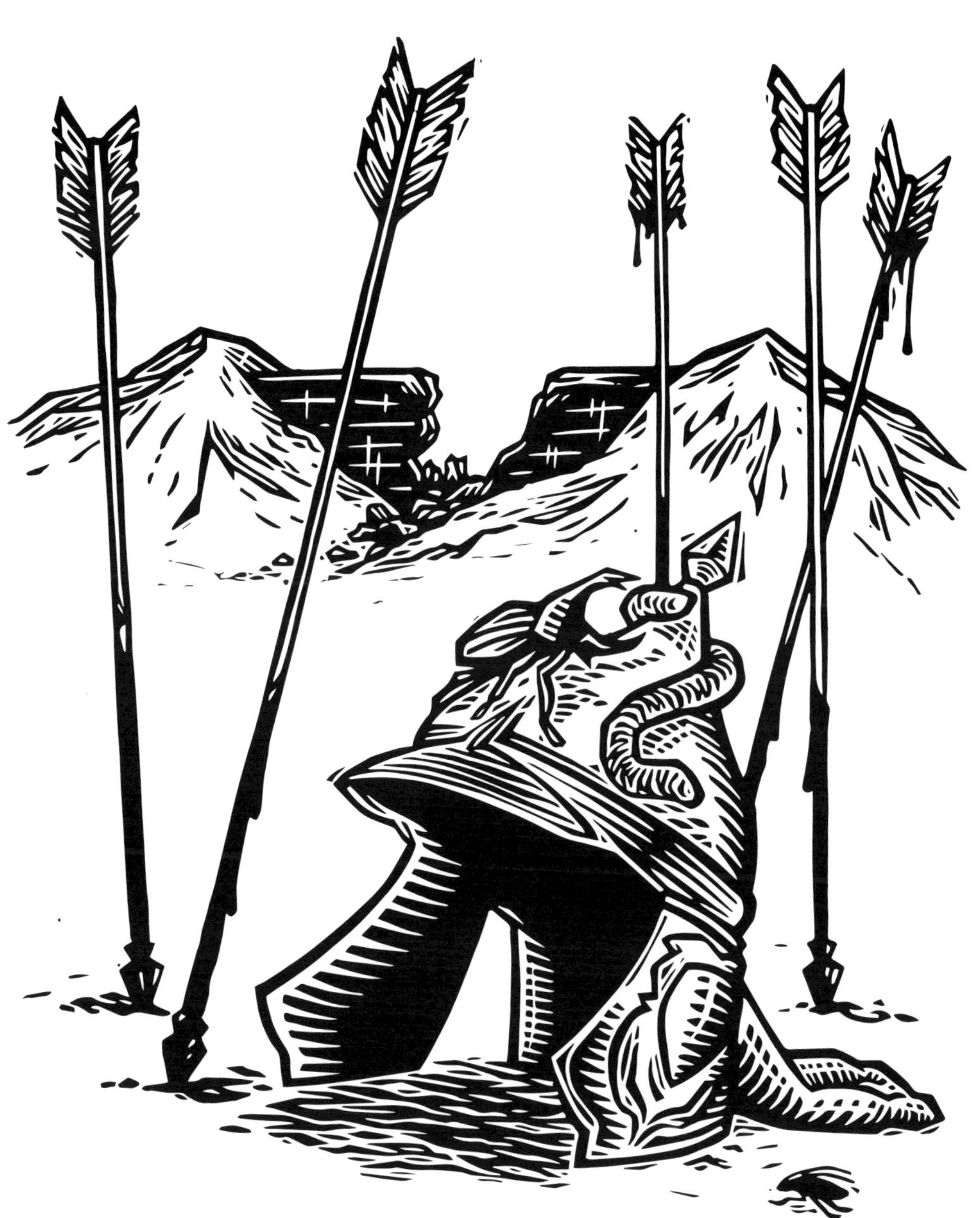

Extermination

Reflecting a natural fear of the unknown, tribes throughout history have been hostile to outsiders. A community can't have a unified idea of "us" without a counterpart "them." Entire civilizations have been wiped out just by coming in contact with another. Highly developed societies of the Bronze Age came to a violent collapse by invasions, causing centuries of economic, intellectual, and cultural regression known as the Dark Ages. Conflict often arises between tribes under the pretense of cultural, religious, or genetic superiority.

About a thousand years ago, trade routes connecting Africa, Asia, and Europe became communication highways for sharing inventions, art, language, religion, and customs. With advanced commerce and wealth came transcontinental war and the dawn of white supremacy. A racial tier system was developed and tied to trade roles, with white Europeans on top. Darker-skinned Africans were in the bottom tier, negating their rights to property. One can only rationalize enslaving people by viewing them as subhuman creatures. Eventually this view was brought to the Americas by settlers, who depicted natives as savages to justify the theft of land and resources. Portraying others as vermin is an effective way to gain public support for inhumane actions.

Many ethnicities have been targeted for genocide all over the world, including the Circassians in Russia, Jews by the Nazis, Cambodians by the Khmer Rouge, and the Tutsis in Rwanda. Any group of people can be victimized once they've been collectively dehumanized by the people in power.

Power dynamics shift over time. Whether you're part of a community that has been the exterminator or the exterminated, it's worth noting that the point of the blade can always turn around. When given the opportunity to value others while having authority, our actions prove the true strength of a society.

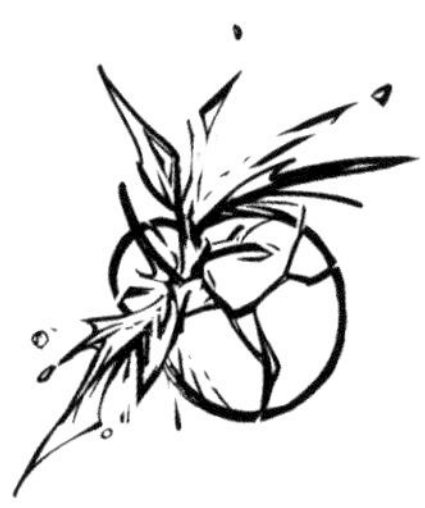

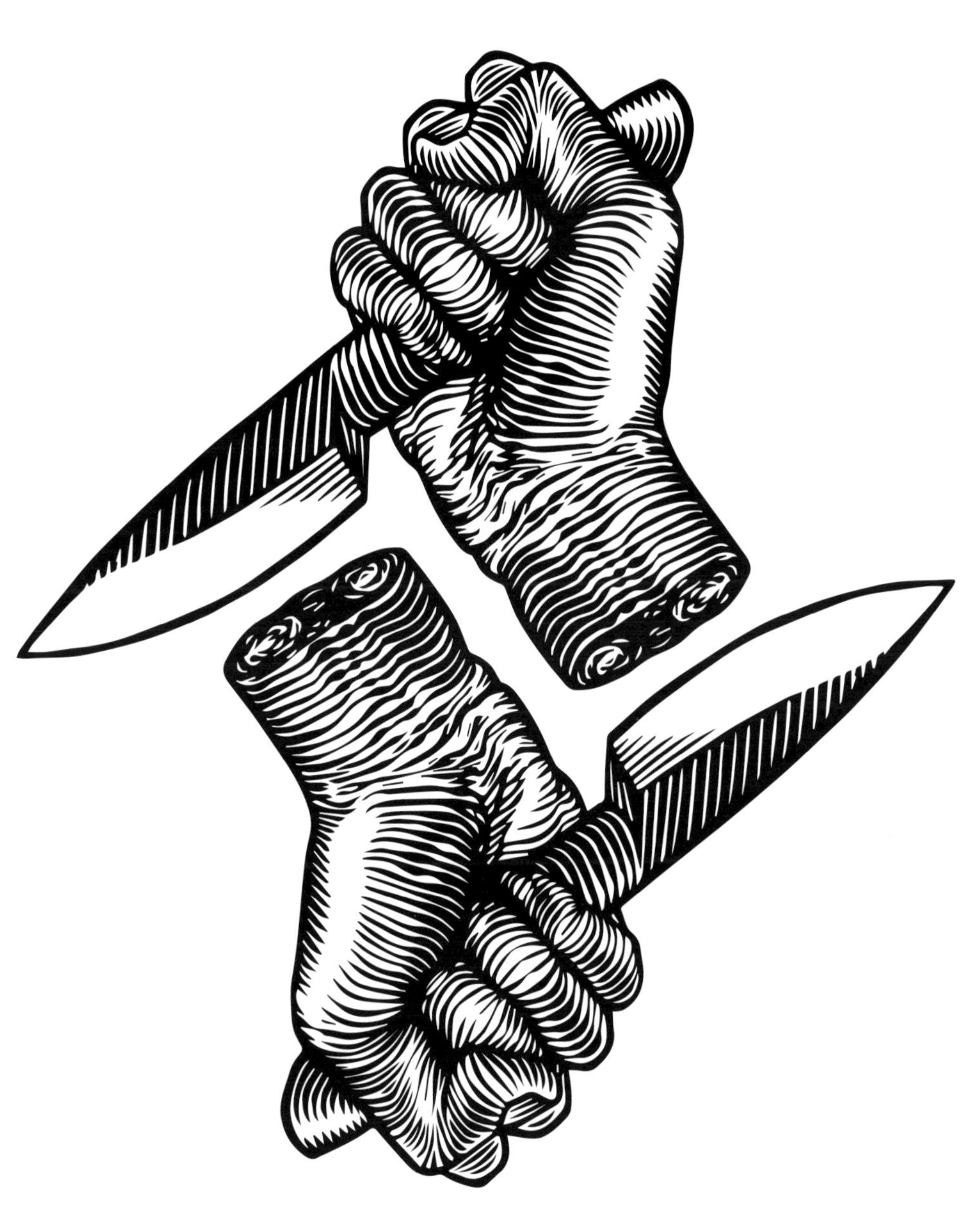

Ragnarök

In the final chapter of Norse mythology, there is a cataclysmic destruction of the universe. Known as Ragnarök, meaning "Fate of the Gods," it reflects how the battle-obsessed Vikings of the thirteenth century viewed the world in their time.

Ragnarök begins with a great winter that brings biting winds and icy snow for three years. The resulting hardship spreads war across the land, pinning brother against brother and father against son.

Fenrir, a giant wolf with fiery eyes, is released from his chains and sets out to destroy everything in his path. Ruler god Odin and his champion warriors are foretold they're certain to lose the battle, but still they pursue Fenrir. The outcome of the world depends on them. They fight valiantly and are eventually swallowed by the beast.

Jormungand, a mighty serpent that dwells at the bottom of the ocean, finally rises from the depths to battle Thor, creator of lightning. Although the warrior god defeats Jormungand with his powerful hammer, he is weakened by the serpent's venom and suffers an agonizing death.

The remains of the world sink into the sea. The mythical wolves that forever hunt the sun and moon finally catch their prey, devouring the stars along with them, leaving nothing but a black void.

This tragic ending can be demoralizing, but most Vikings interpreted the tale as motivation to lead a life filled with honor and courage. If heroic gods can confront inevitable pain and loss, then there's no reason for any of us to live paralyzed by fear.

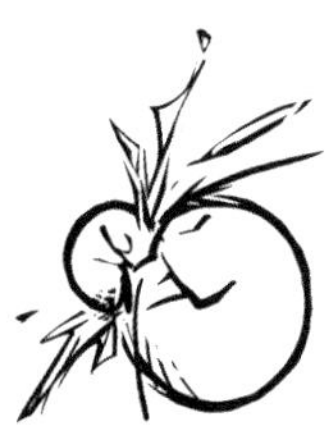

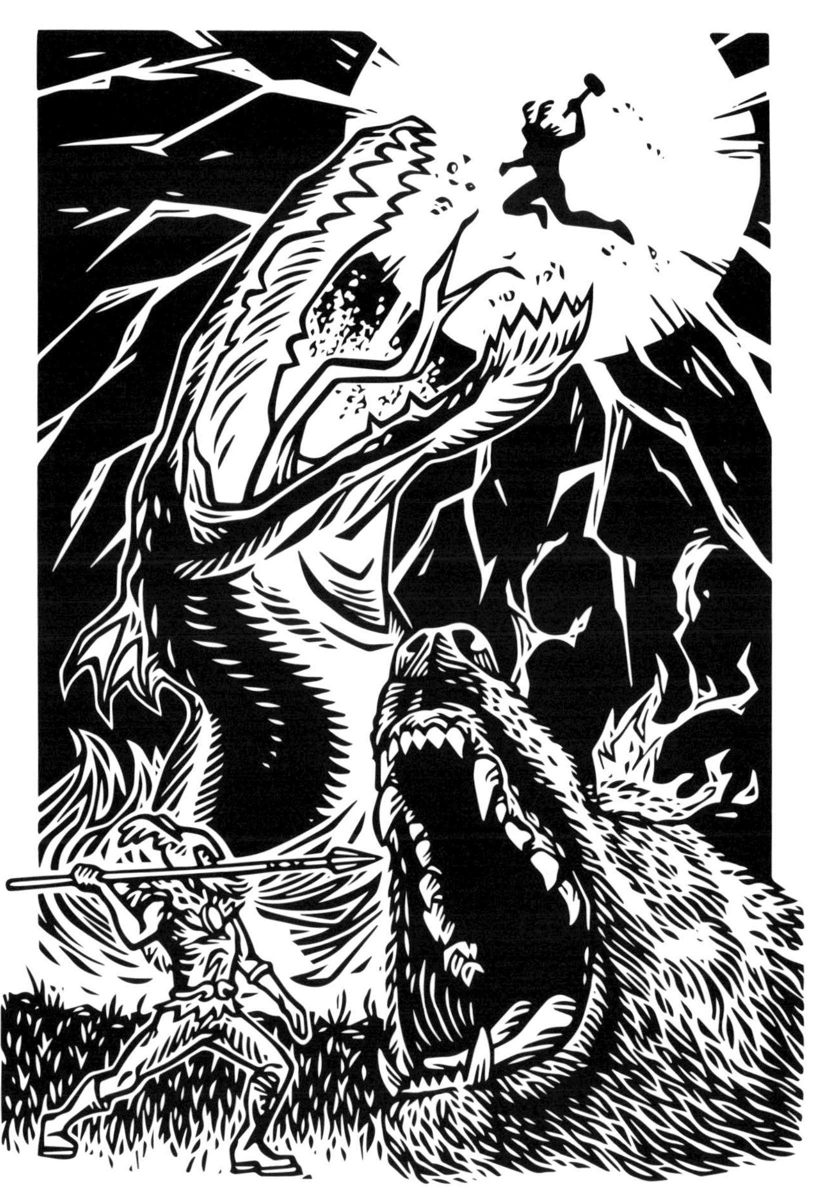

Plague

Five thousand years ago, civilizations began to gather, trade, and travel at rapidly accelerating rates. Since then, the spread of contagious disease has been a constant threat to humanity. Fortunately, our understanding of science has grown as rapidly as the scourge of sickness.

The Black Death swept across Europe in the fourteenth century. As agriculture and skilled crafts improved, people were looking for convenient hubs of commerce. City populations exploded, and commodities weren't the only things being shared. These densely populated areas became the ideal hosts to scavenger rodents, which carried fleas, which transmitted deadly bacteria. This was long before the recognition of germs and hygiene, so there was little hope to curb the spread of disease. Within six years, the bubonic plague wiped out up to 60 percent of the European population. Some doctors knew at the time to cover their faces with masks, while others cautioned against preventative measures. They declared the disease was sent by God, so death would ensure a place in paradise.

Today, our understanding of viruses has improved but we're more vulnerable than ever. Urban sprawl has expanded into wildlife habitats, exposing humans to diseases carried by animals we wouldn't normally come in contact with. The COVID-19 pandemic has proven that modern science has an incredible ability to react to these ancient problems, but until we limit human contact with animal-hosted viruses, a worse one could be right around the corner.

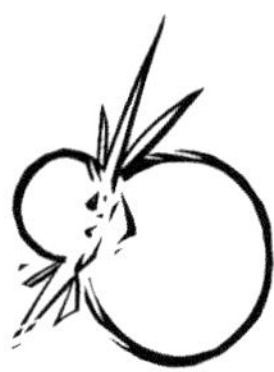

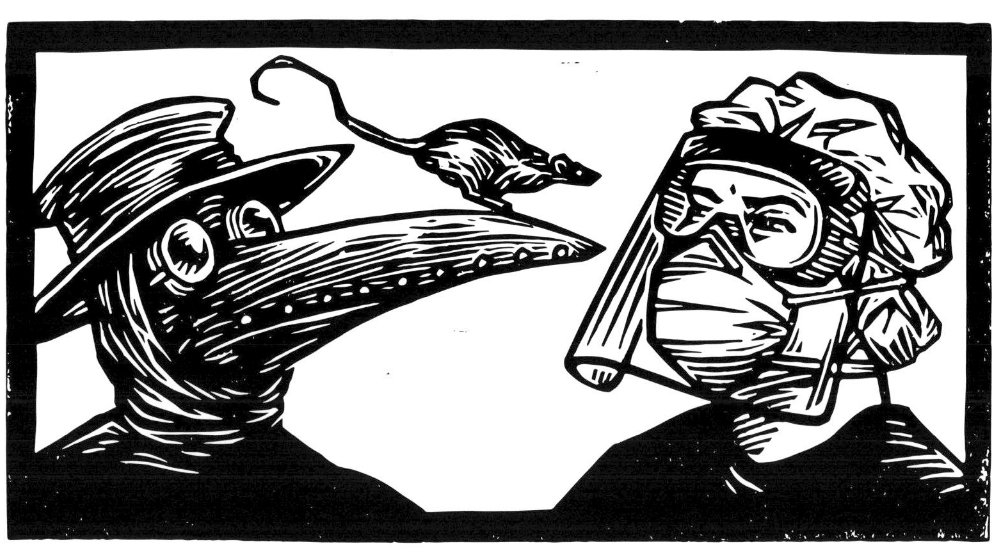

Namazu, the Earthshaker

Earthquakes are localized events that couldn't alone demolish the entire planet. The people of fifteenth-century Japan didn't know that, however, when they began sharing stories of a giant catfish named Namazu that lives under the islands and wreaks havoc on surface-dwellers by thrashing its tail. The myth also includes warrior god Kashima, who eternally tries to pin Namazu in place with a magical balancing stone. It's only when Kashima slips that the mighty fish writhes free and rattles the world.

Japan is one of the most apocalyptic places on the planet. Sitting atop two shifting tectonic plates, the island nation experiences about ten percent of all seismic activity on Earth. The underground rustling causes relentless earthquakes, volcanic eruptions, and tsunamis. The legend of Namazu has given people a way to explain these seemingly arbitrary disasters.

Long ago, fishermen noticed catfish rising from their watery depths shortly before earthquakes struck. Stories were shared and the slippery forecasters became the subject of an oral tradition that continues to evolve today. The catfish is a serpentine symbol for mischief but also has the ability to ward off danger. People place stones at shrines to create balance and prevent earthquakes, just like Kashima. Displaying catfish art at home represents a sturdy household and invites a steady renewal of the spirit. Namazu and its natural disasters may bring destruction and despair, but they are also credited with granting the world a continuous life cycle and the opportunity to start anew.

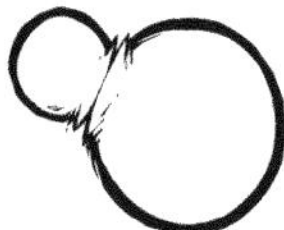

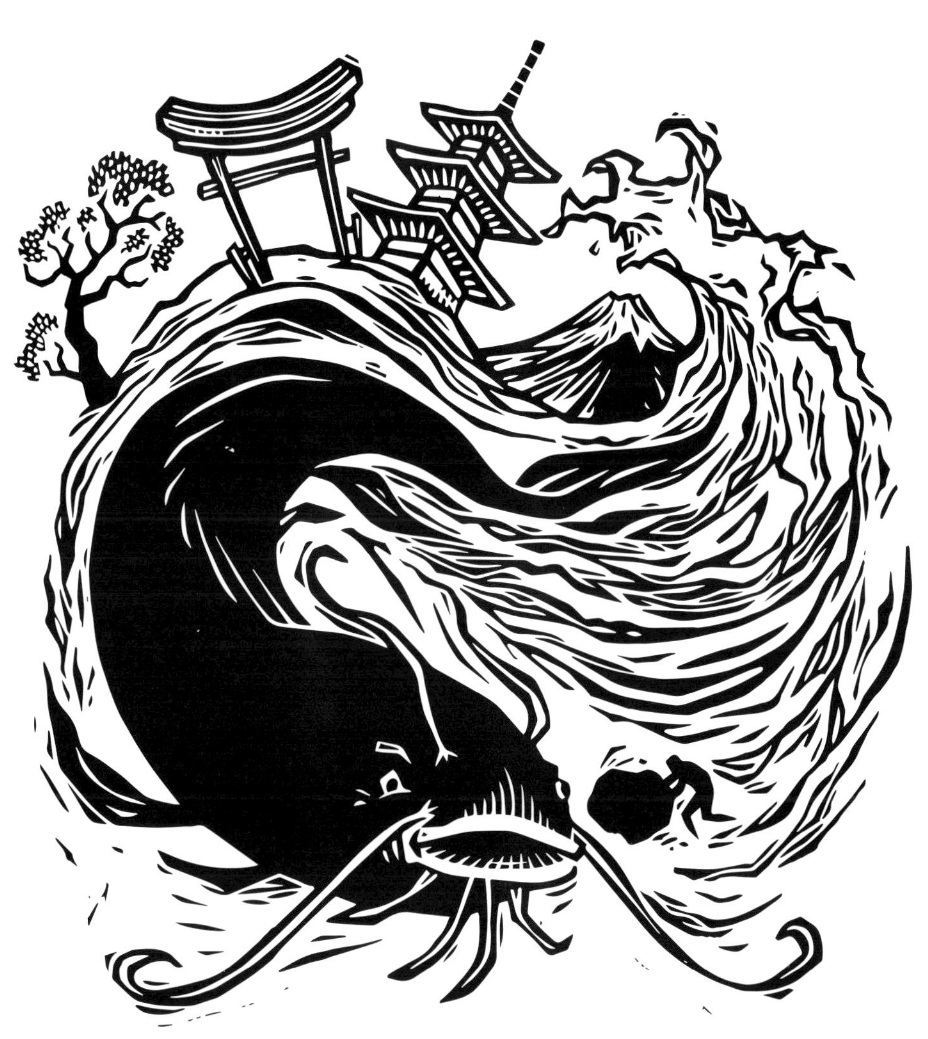

Stöffler's Flood

It can be frustrating when your local meteorologist gets the weather forecast wrong. You may not get that day off you were hoping for. You might get stuck in an unexpected storm and be severely inconvenienced. Now imagine your disappointment if you had to keep on living after you'd been convinced that everyone would die by flood.

Johannes Stöffler was a renowned German astronomer, mathematician, inventor, priest, and apocalyptic meteorologist. His calculations observed that on February 20, 1524, most of the six known planets would align. More than a coincidence that we now know happens about every century, Stöffler decided it must be the most consequential event imaginable: the end of the world. Astronomy and astrology were intertwined at the time and 1524 was a Pisces year, so he envisioned the water sign would bring a flood engulfing much of the land on Earth.

Stöffler was the head of mathematics and first professor of astronomy at the prestigious University of Tübingen, so his claims were not easily dismissed. As his prophecy neared, panic spread across Germany and beyond. Londoners fled the city for high ground. Churches were turned into fortresses. Boat builders and emergency supply merchants became saviors.

On February 20, 1524, it rained. People fled to the Rhine in an attempt to board any boat available. A German noble had an extravagant ark built to survive the flood in style, but it didn't protect him from desperate commoners. He died along with hundreds of others in the chaos on the river. The rain stopped well short of a flood, but the damage was done. Stöffler had sullied his good name and lived out his days in shame until he died by plague. Despite his positive contributions to the world, his miscalculations caused death and hysteria along with public distrust of science and astrology.

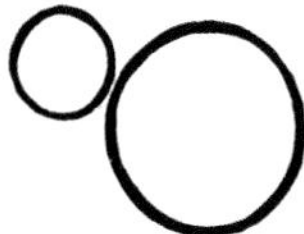

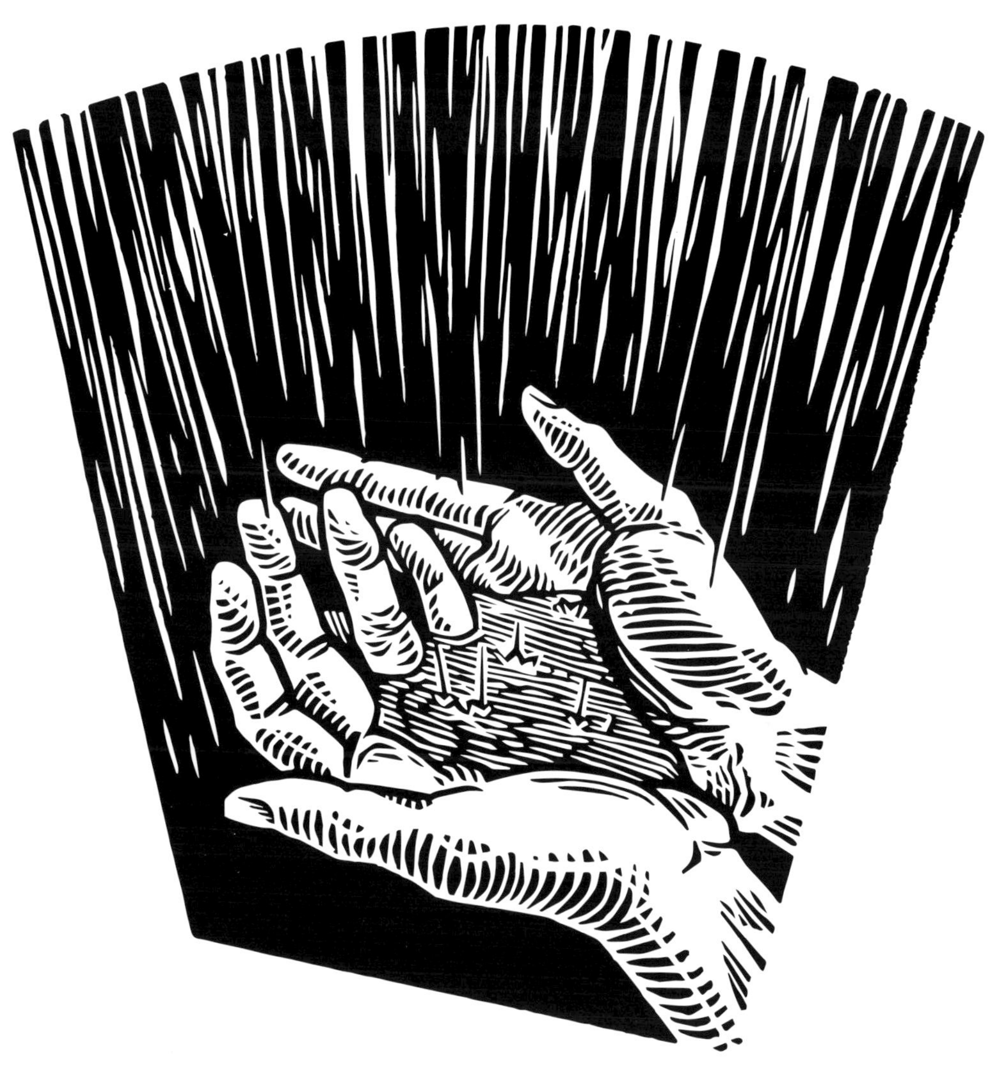

Doomsday Cults

Being a follower of a cult shows incredible commitment. To be a leader of a cult, one must find a compelling way to take advantage of this dedication. By convincing supporters that the end is coming, they will have nothing else to live for and can then fully devote themselves to the cause.

In the sixteenth century, a German mystic named Melchior Hofmann declared himself a divine witness of the forthcoming end times. He traveled town to town, gathering excitable and violent followers who called themselves Melchiorites after their leader. They drew attention for sparking political, social, and religious unrest. Hofmann was eventually imprisoned for their disturbances, leaving a mob of bloodthirsty devotees with no one to follow.

Luckily, the movement soon found Jan Matthys, another leader claiming to be capable of foreseeing the apocalypse. In 1534, after years of being chased out of villages, the group seized control of the tolerant and peaceful town of Münster. They forced baptisms and marriages on citizens. Money, property, and Catholicism were punishable by death. Matthys reportedly decapitated one of his sixteen wives because she insinuated that his lifestyle had grown too extravagant.

Word spread of the extremists, and an intervening army set up a blockade around the city walls. As supplies and food dwindled, a confident Matthys prophesied that God's judgment would fall upon the wicked. He was correct. After a short battle, his severed head and genitals were displayed at the city gate. Münster is now known as a thriving university town full of friendly bicyclists, but they still hang human-sized cages that once held the bodies of doomsday cult leaders.

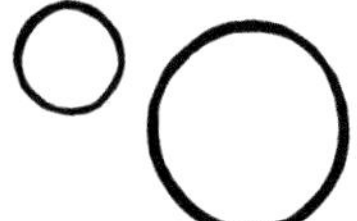

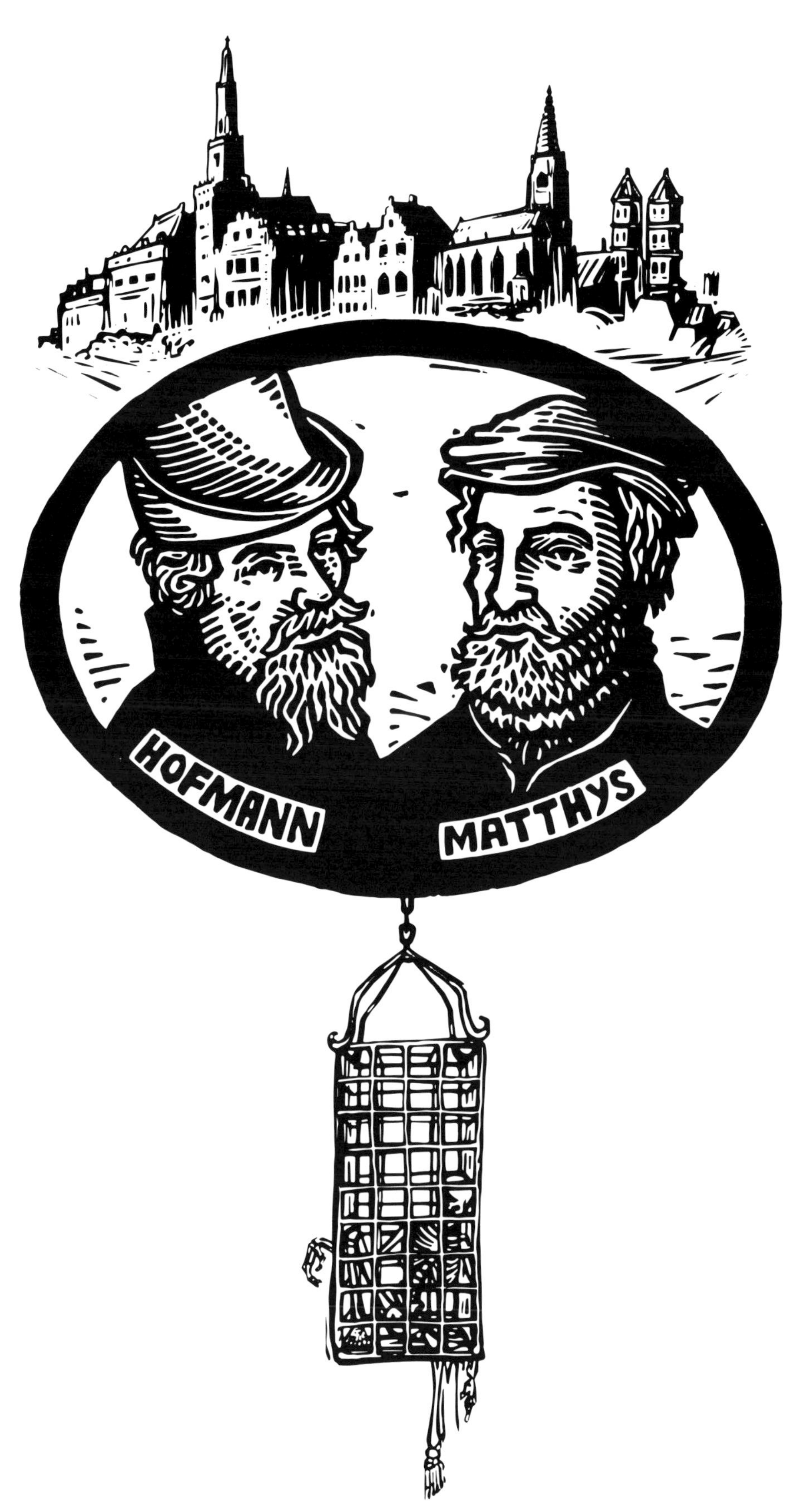
HOFMANN
MATTHYS

American Baptist preacher William Miller announced that Christ would return on October 22, 1844. In the years leading up to the event, his prophecy grew from a regional movement in upstate New York to a national campaign with weekly updates in local newspapers. His enthusiastic mass of followers, known as Millerites, gave away their earthly possessions and awaited the Advent, when they'd be lifted into Heaven and leave the naysayers behind.

When the day passed without incident, heartbroken Millerites were mocked in the street. Some were merely teased and asked if they lost their tickets to Heaven. Others were attacked, such as a group in Toronto that were tarred and feathered. A congregation in Illinois was ambushed by a mob wielding clubs and knives. For disillusioned Millerites in New York, shame turned to anger as they burned down their own churches. The woeful repercussions for this error in judgment came to be known as the Great Disappointment—a phrase that could be used to describe many things.

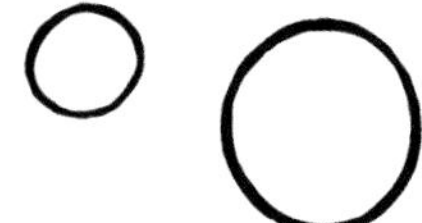

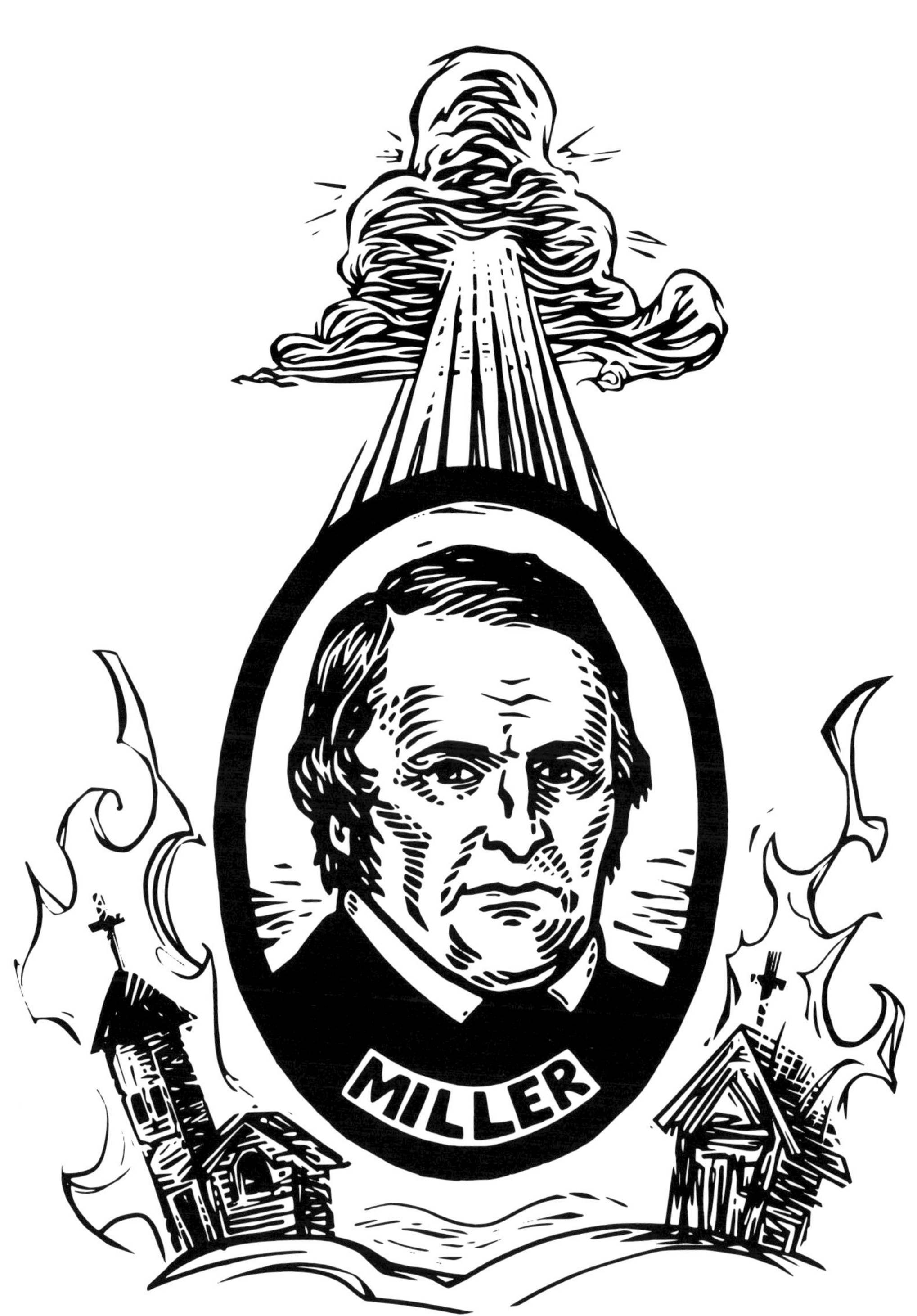
MILLER

South African evangelist Enoch Mgijima predicted the world would end on Christmas Day of 1912. Even after the prophecy proved false and he was excommunicated by the church, his new attention attracted thousands of followers.

Mgijima saw visions while hunting game, and he said the spirit of God insisted he share it with the world. He once described a prescient dream of two goats fighting while a baboon looked on. He interpreted this as a war between whites that didn't involve black Africans, which he later claimed was a prediction of World War I.* His recurring visions of a world overrun by violence convinced his followers to stop working their own land and dedicate themselves to a secluded settlement in the mountains, where they awaited the coming of the Lord.

When the rapidly expanding outpost was discovered by a British landlord, tensions arose between Mgijima and the government. Mgijima saw little need for taxes and registration when the end of the world was surely just on the horizon. After years of failed negotiations, police decided to remove the group by force in 1921. Armed with machine guns and heavy artillery, the government moved swiftly on the ill-equipped colony. In twenty minutes, 163 religious followers were killed in the tragic event now known as the Bulhoek massacre. Mgijima was imprisoned and worked hard labor until his death in 1928.

* However, many black Africans did fight in the First World War, including in the East African Campaign.

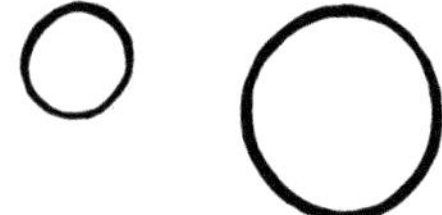

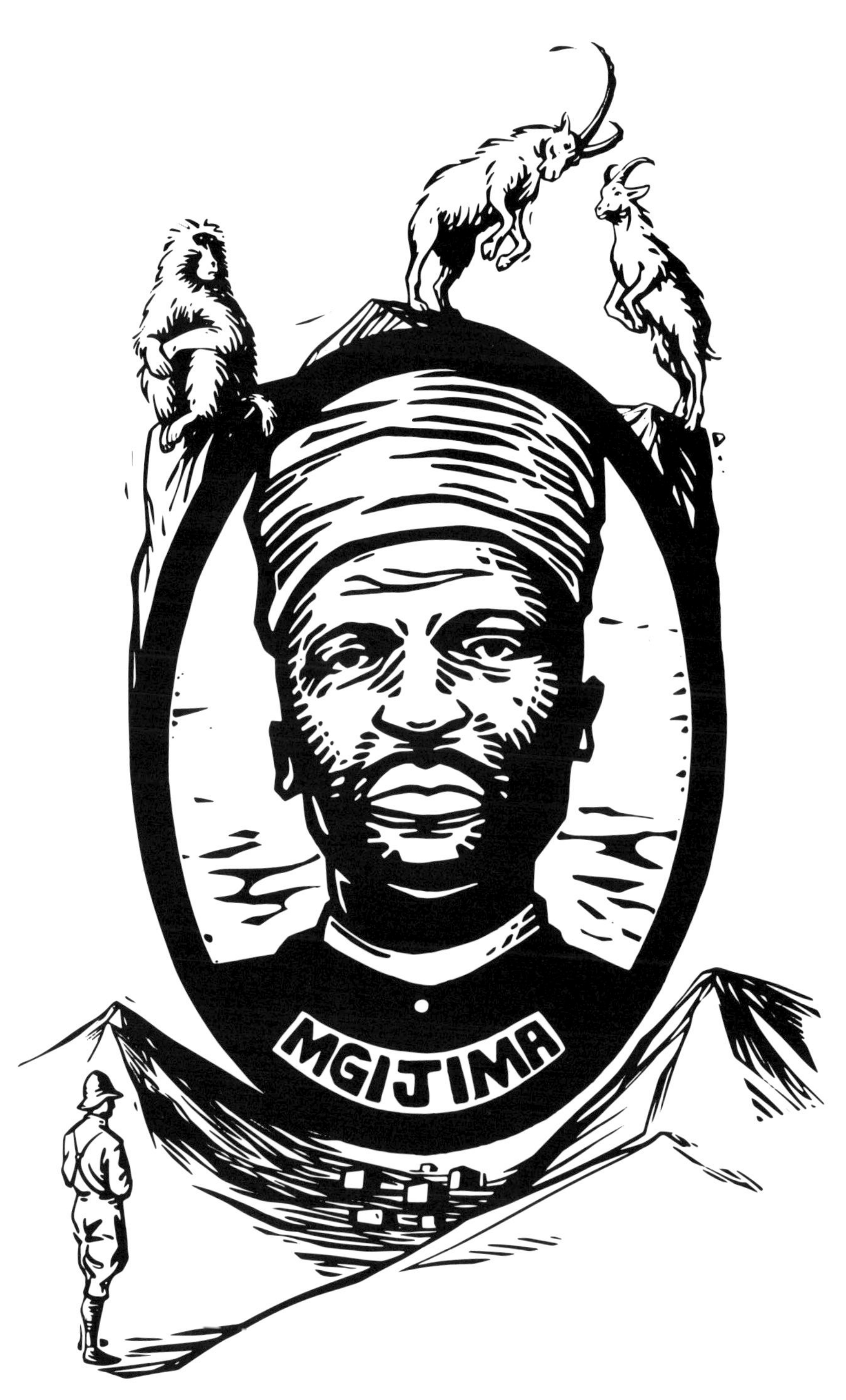
MGIJIMA

Jim Jones was a charismatic preacher who claimed to have psychic powers to see the future and heal the sick. In 1955, he founded his own church in Indiana that promoted racial unity during a time of staunch segregation. People were slow to join his radical church, known as the Peoples Temple, so he worked as a door-to-door monkey salesman to make ends meet. As the church grew, so did Jones' obsession with nuclear war. He preached that a nuclear apocalypse would occur on July 15, 1967. He moved the church to California, where he said they would be safe from the bombs.

The apocalypse failed to materialize, but Jones' paranoia got worse as an addiction to pills began to unravel his charm. He separated families, asserting power over women and claiming every man on Earth except him was a homosexual. Faced with accusations of extortion, drug abuse, and sexual assault, Jones decided to relocate again. Members of the Temple sold their belongings and moved to South America, along with their chimpanzee mascot, Mr. Muggs.

In Guyana, Jones established a private commune called Jonestown. He renamed himself "the Prophet" and exercised control over his followers by confiscating passports and money. The compound was protected by armed guards to prevent members from escaping. Jones was also at war with the outside world, leading to the killing of a California congressman who came to Jonestown looking to free members from the Temple.

On November 18, 1978, Jones persuaded nine hundred followers to commit suicide by drinking cyanide-laced punch. The tragedy birthed the phrase "drinking the Kool-Aid," which is still used to describe the act of foolishly following something. Neither Jones nor Mr. Muggs survived.

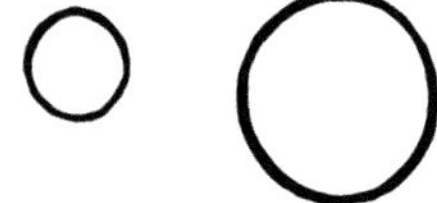

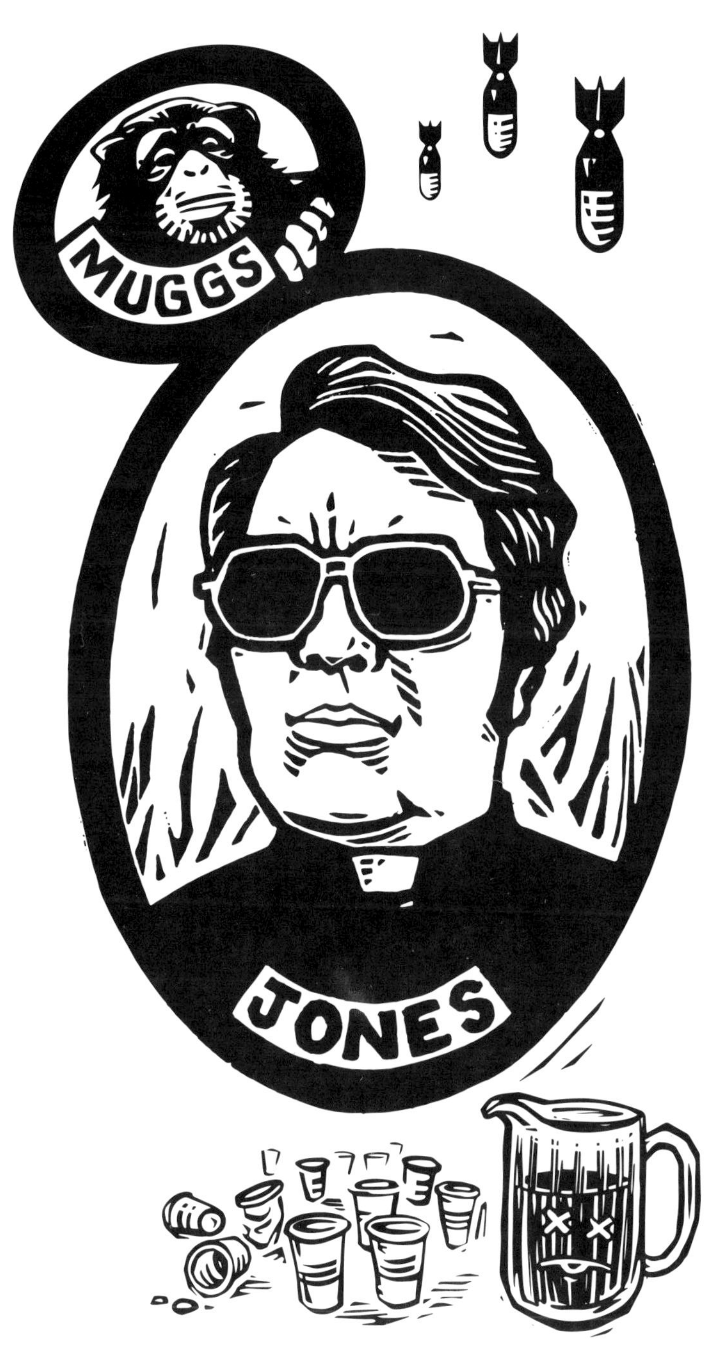

MUGGS
JONES

Charles Manson spoke about a "Helter Skelter" scenario in which an apocalyptic war would arise from racial tensions between black and white people. In the 1960s, after years spent in and out of prison, the former pimp and aspiring singer-songwriter turned his attention to the counterculture movement blossoming in California. Manson found that uninhibited drug-fueled hippies could be easily manipulated into helping him gain wealth, fame, and power. He met people in Satanist circles, where he compiled a group of followers known as the Manson Family. He spoke incessantly about death and murder, gradually growing impatient for Helter Skelter to begin.

In 1969, Manson ordered followers to go on a killing spree throughout Los Angeles. At the crime scenes, they wrote "Helter Skelter" in blood, accompanying demonic and racially charged messages in a staged attempt to appear like the apocalyptic war had begun. The ritualistic murders set off a wave of fear and distrust of neighbors, contributing to the end of the free love era in America. Manson finally gained the fame and notoriety he craved, but would spend the rest of his life in prison.

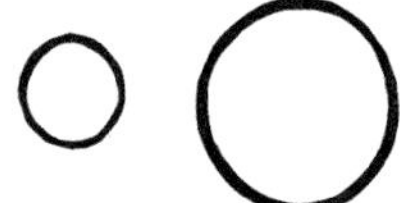

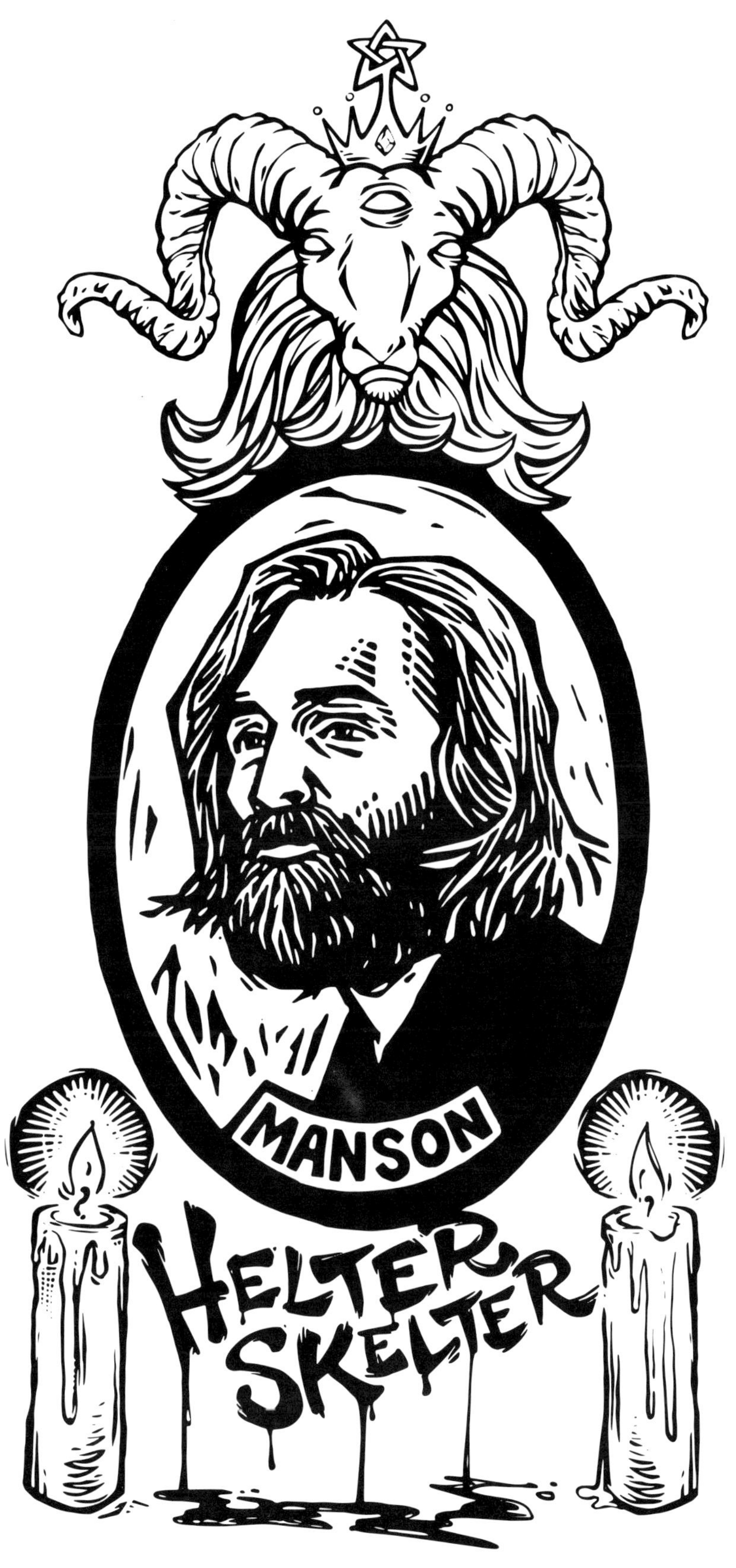
MANSON
HELTER SKELTER

Sometimes, you need to bring the apocalypse upon yourself. In Waco, Texas, David Koresh claimed to be the final prophet of his Branch Davidian movement. Followers believed they were living in the end times and that their Christian commune, known as Ranch Apocalypse, would be the center of a new divine kingdom. Koresh preached about the nearing Armageddon, in which he was an angel warrior facing persecution in a reign of hellfire. "If the Bible is true, then I'm Christ," he said on more than one occasion.

In 1993, newspapers dubbed Koresh "The Sinful Messiah" in an article reporting child abuse and statutory rape of his multiple underage brides. The next day, the federal government attempted to execute a search warrant on the compound to investigate a stash of illegal firearms. A shootout ensued, killing five ATF agents and five Branch Davidians. The government quickly assembled possibly the largest military force ever gathered against civilians in American history. Both sides refused to back down, and a highly publicized fifty-one-day standoff unfolded. Eventually, the government raided the compound with tanks and tear gas, which ignited and set Ranch Apocalypse ablaze in a reign of hellfire. Seventy-six Branch Davidians died in the siege, including twenty-five children and Koresh himself.

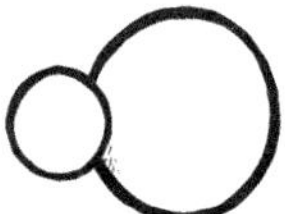

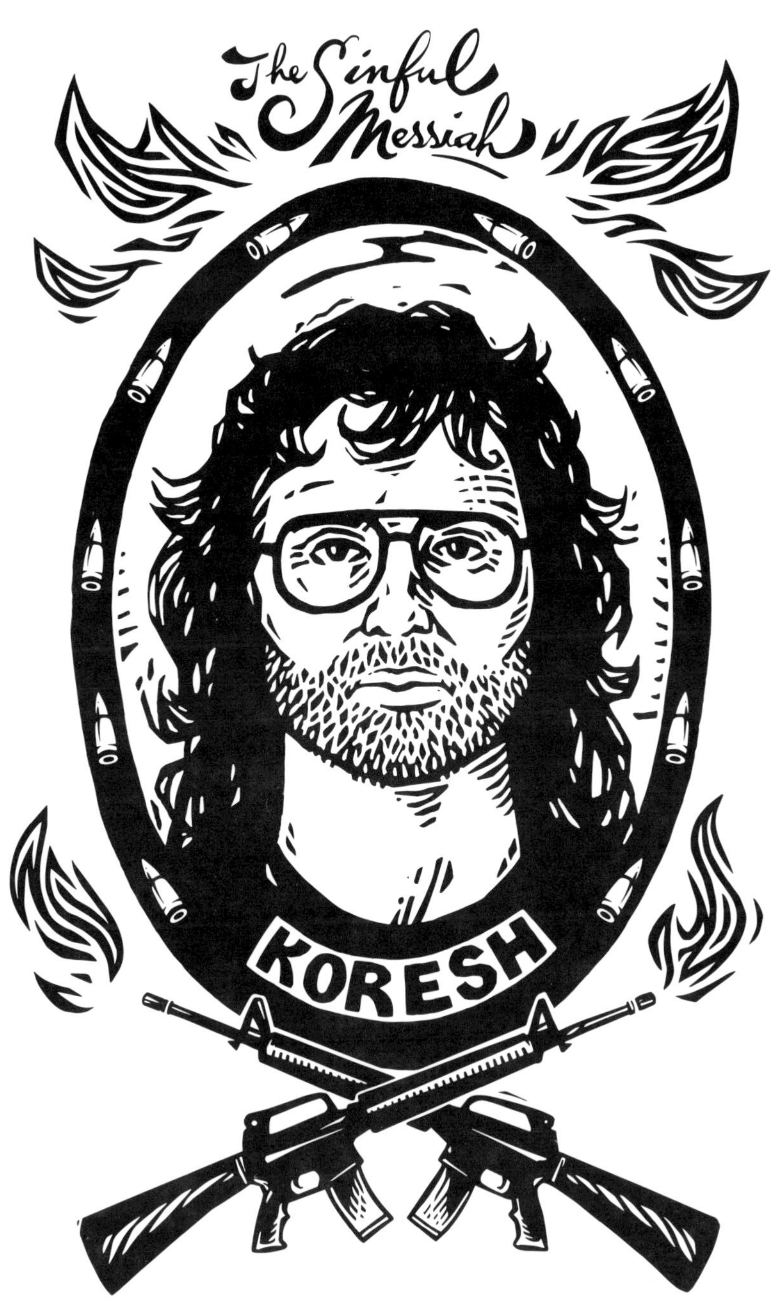
The Sinful Messiah
KORESH

The religious movement Aum Shinrikyo, meaning "Supreme Truth," predicted a nuclear Armageddon brought on by World War III. The prophecy, detailed by founder Shoko Asahara, included a vision of Japan being attacked and Aum Shinrikyo assuming control of the government. He declared that all of humanity would die except for members of the movement.*

A poor blind man from the mountains of Japan, Asahara gained tens of thousands of international followers drawn to his unique combination of high-tech mysticism and apocalyptic yoga. The self-proclaimed guru targeted students under immense pressure at elite universities, promising a more meaningful and less demanding existence. The skills and intellect of his academic outcasts were utilized to construct ultramodern laboratories, where they developed drugs and biological weapons. Fueled by homemade LSD and methamphetamine, followers were taught to reject traditional material items, but were encouraged to spend thousands of dollars to drink Asahara's blood and bathwater.

As Asahara grew more paranoid of the outside world, Aum Shinrikyo began to kidnap and kill anyone he considered a threat. In 1995, the group coordinated a complex gas attack in a crowded Tokyo subway. Thirteen people died and at least 5,800 were injured in the worst domestic terror attack in Japanese history. Asahara and six Aum members were convicted and eventually executed.

* So act now! This deal won't last!

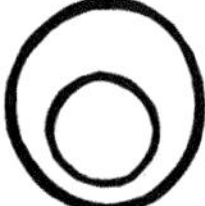

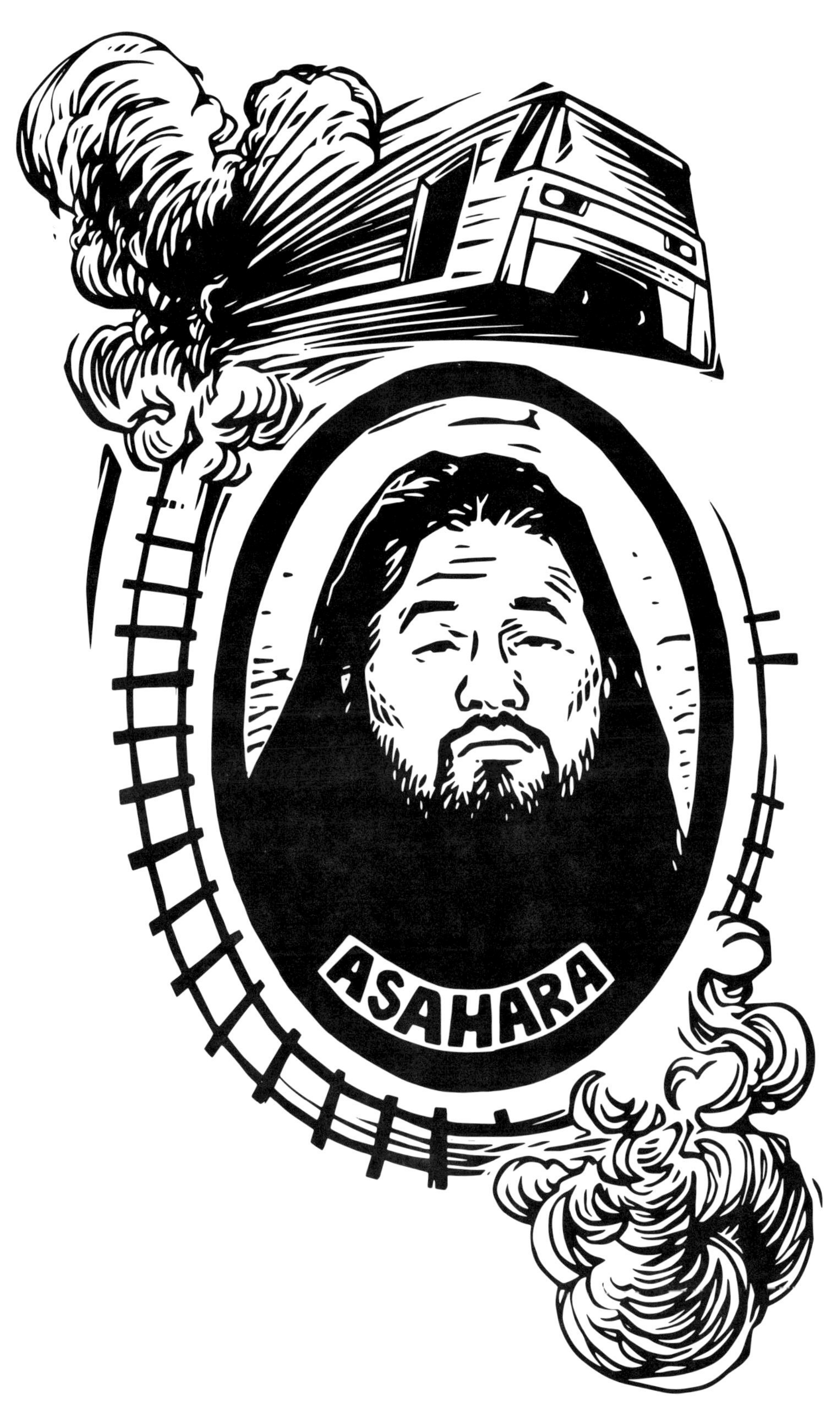
ASAHARA

Heaven's Gate was a UFO religion based around the belief that followers could take part in the rapture and ascend to heaven by transforming into immortal extraterrestrial beings. Group leader Marshall "Do" Applewhite insisted they use coded names, assimilate appearances, and obey strict rules of the household. Members gave Do their life savings to pay for classes and alien abduction insurance. Their contributions also paid for a $30,000 full-page ad in *USA Today* warning people of the catastrophic judgment set to befall Earth. Everyone in Heaven's Gate renounced their human identities for a chance to be accepted by aliens. In an attempt to scrub all human programming from their brains and bodies, some male members, including Do, castrated themselves.

On March 26, 1997, after decades of preparation, Do was ready to transform and leave his human vessel behind. Participants gathered in California, dressed in matching Nike sneakers and clothes with "Heaven's Gate Away Team" patches. Thirty-nine people ate poisoned applesauce and died in an attempt to evacuate Earth. Nike capitalized on the attention with collectible "Heaven's Gate" Dunk High Pro SB Premium sneakers, now worth thousands of dollars to faithful sneakerheads and cult heads alike.

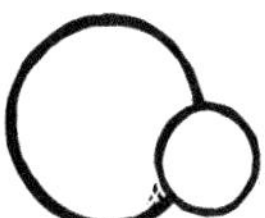

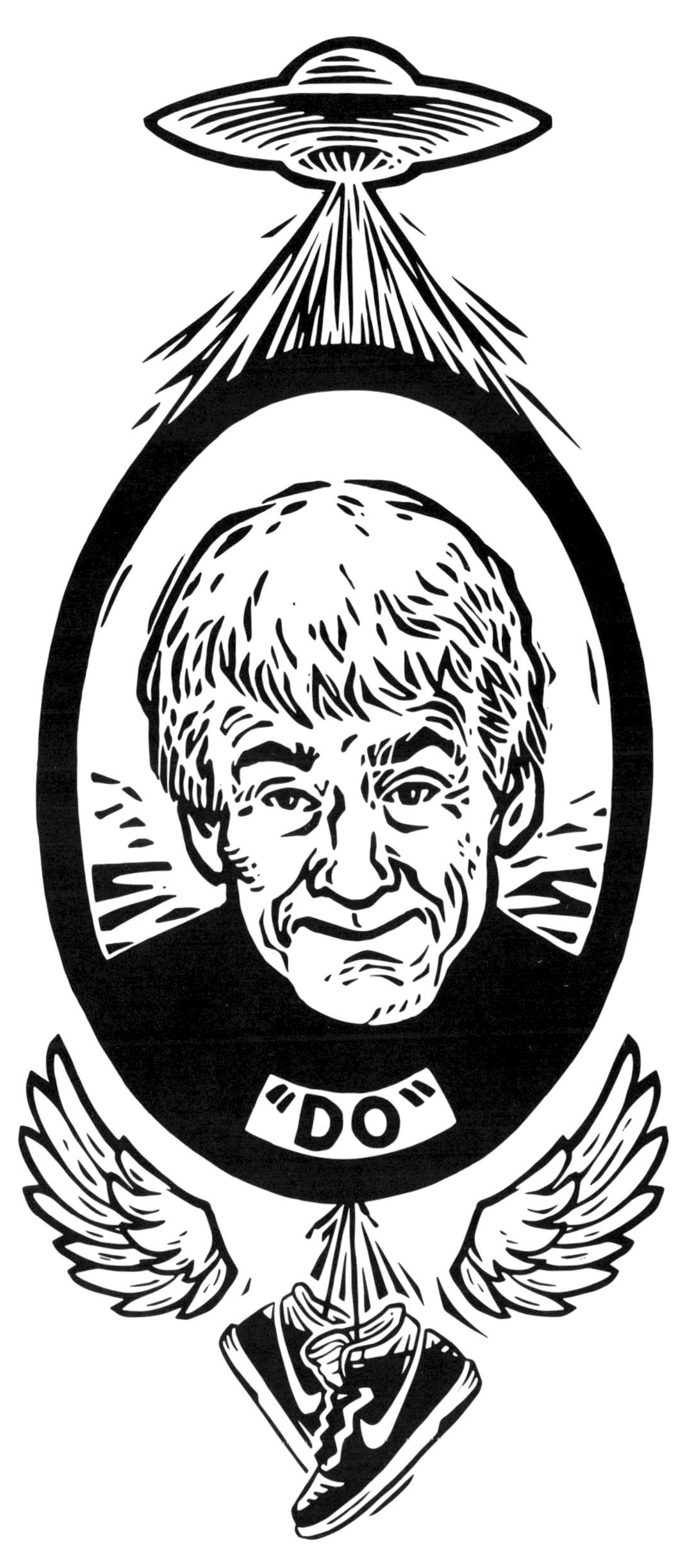

"DO"

In 1997, about 150 followers of the church of Chen Tao, or "True Way," arrived in Texas from Taiwan. Asia had been experiencing an economic crisis, enormous wildfires, and fear of nuclear annihilation. Chen Tao considered these events a prelude to larger disaster. Of all places to hide out, they reportedly chose Garland, Texas as their destination because the name sounded like "God's Land." Locals of Garland immediately warmed to their quiet, pleasant new neighbors. Composed of affluent doctors, engineers, and teachers, the members of Chen Tao spoke of a spiritual connection with technology. Their leader, Teacher Chen, was a former social science professor who claimed to have fathered Jesus Christ 2,000 years ago. Having recently discovered the reincarnation of Christ in a ten-year-old boy, they were prepared for the apocalypse.

Chen prophesied that God would announce his arrival by broadcasting Himself on channel 18 of all television sets around the world. Then, on March 31, 1998, at 10 a.m., God would take the form of Chen's body, signaling the end of their time on Earth. A flying saucer would arrive to bring them to Heaven, possibly with a stop at Mars along the way.

When God did not appear, a remorseful Chen offered himself to be executed, stoned to death, or crucified. Instead, the peaceful followers chose to dissolve the church and move on. They have not been heard from since.

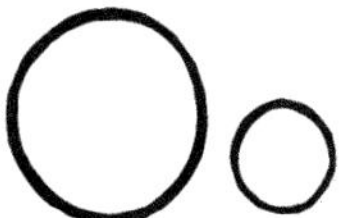

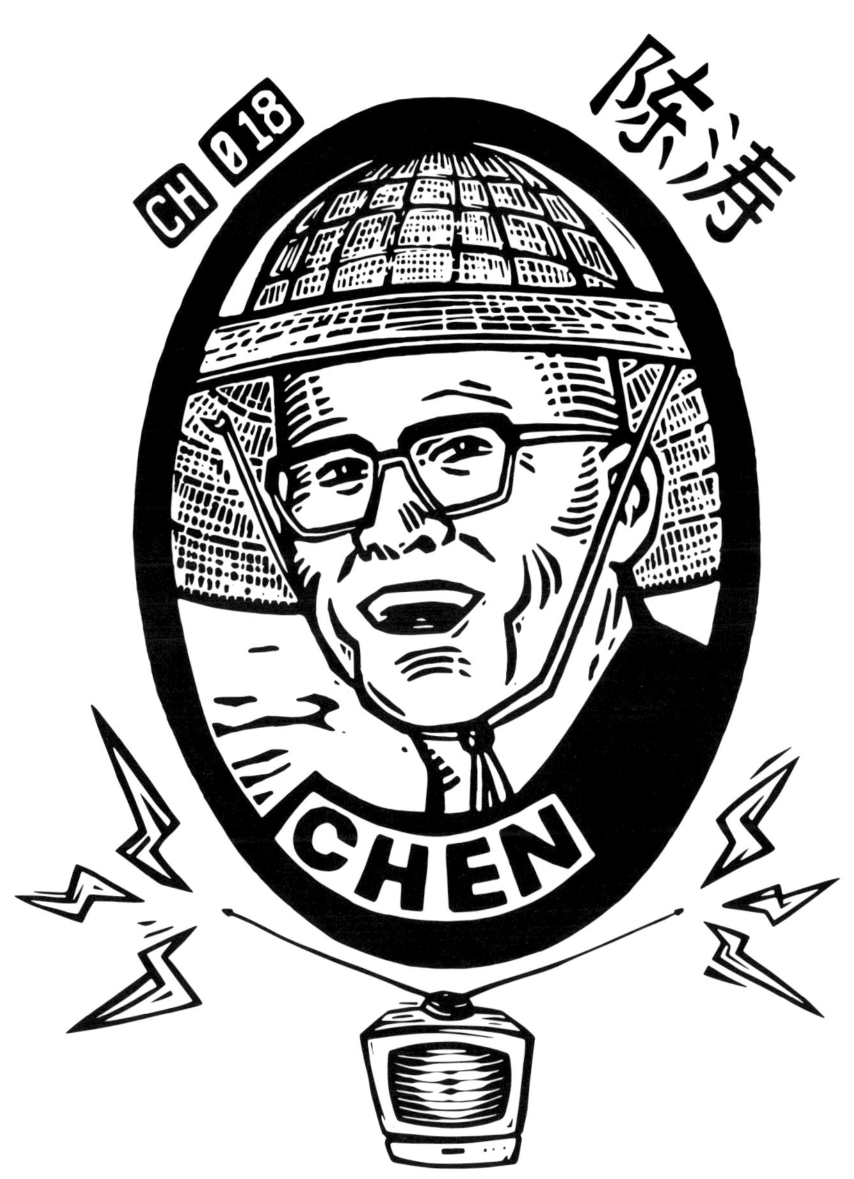
CH 018
陈涛
CHEN

In the modern age of the internet, we still can't quit the doomsday cult. Survivalist blogger James Rawles convinces followers of an impending economic collapse that will destroy civilization. His proposed solution includes forming well-armed militias in the countryside.

The political group QAnon, led by mysterious internet idol "Q," unites people through a fear of the American government and the deep state. Watching for impending doomsday events plays a major role in keeping followers galvanized, with trajectories and deadlines to track. They're regularly warned that a "storm is coming," as they wait patiently for politicians to be arrested, elections to be overturned, or evidence to be unveiled of Satan-worshipping child sex traffickers. When nothing happens, they return to the web in search of future great disappointments.

There will always be a desire to be led by someone who is confidently knowledgeable about all the things we're uncertain of. It's a harsh world to face alone, but the even harsher reality is that no one truly knows what will happen—and certainly not people who name groups after themselves.

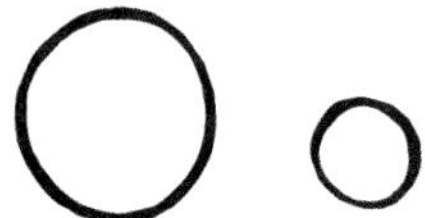

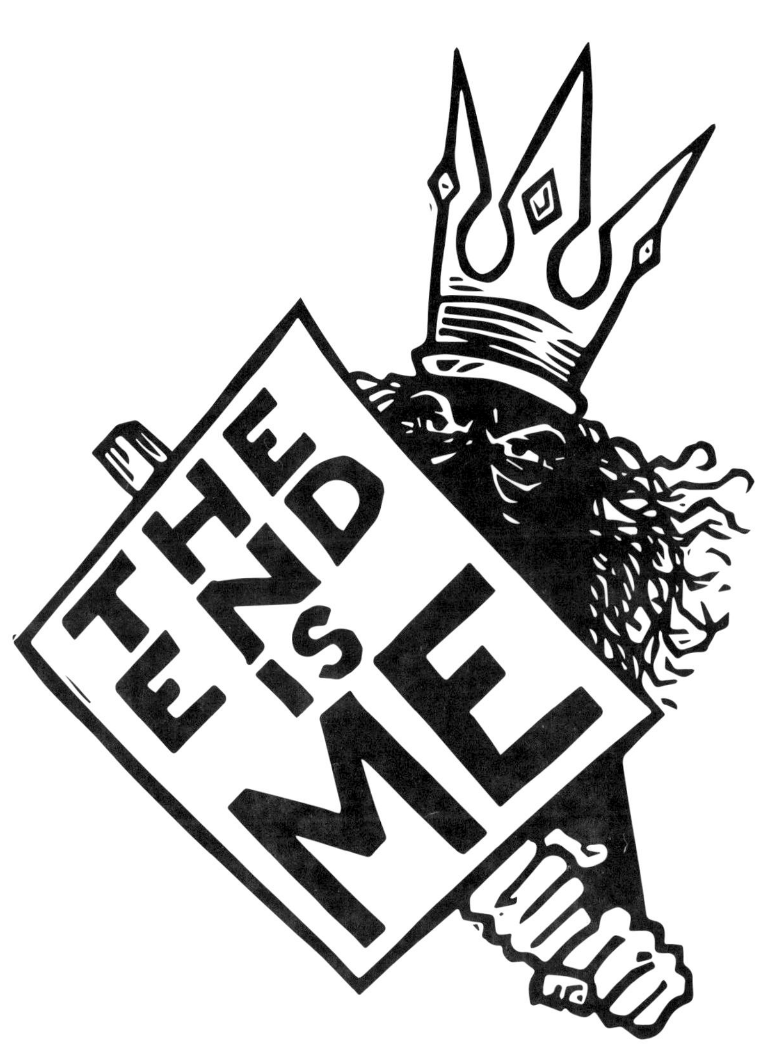

THE END IS ME

Locusts

The prophet Moses once warned an Egyptian pharaoh to obey his instructions or a vengeful God would flood the sky with locusts to "cover each and every tree of the land and eat all that is there to be eaten." Since then, the swarm of locusts has been associated with God smiting the world. So what makes this little bug a nightmarish sign of impending doom?

Locusts are a type of flying grasshopper. They gather and travel long distances in search of plants to eat. What's shocking about these migrations is the sheer number that amass and the magnitude by which they can alter a landscape. A single swarm of locusts can count in the tens of billions, and they descend as dark clouds upon vast expanses of land to ravage all vegetation. It's no surprise that someone, especially a victimized farmer, might think they're witnessing a coming apocalypse.

When early colonists arrived in North America in the seventeenth century, they were greeted by billions of little flying monstrosities. Familiar with Moses' warning, the colonists thought they were experiencing the wrath of God. There was a devilish humming that permeated the air as the bugs emerged from underground dwellings and rendezvoused in trees. Their distinct red eyes were said to be forged in the depths of Hell. It turns out locusts don't have red eyes, so their accounts of unholy tormentors could not have been a punishment from the Almighty. The colonists had been visited by the harmless cicada, which congregates above ground every seventeen years to breed loudly in trees and annoy humans into thinking the world will end.

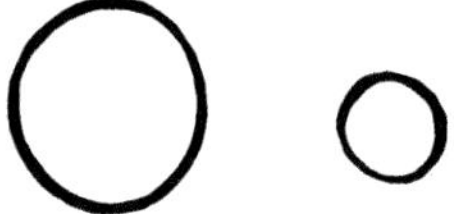

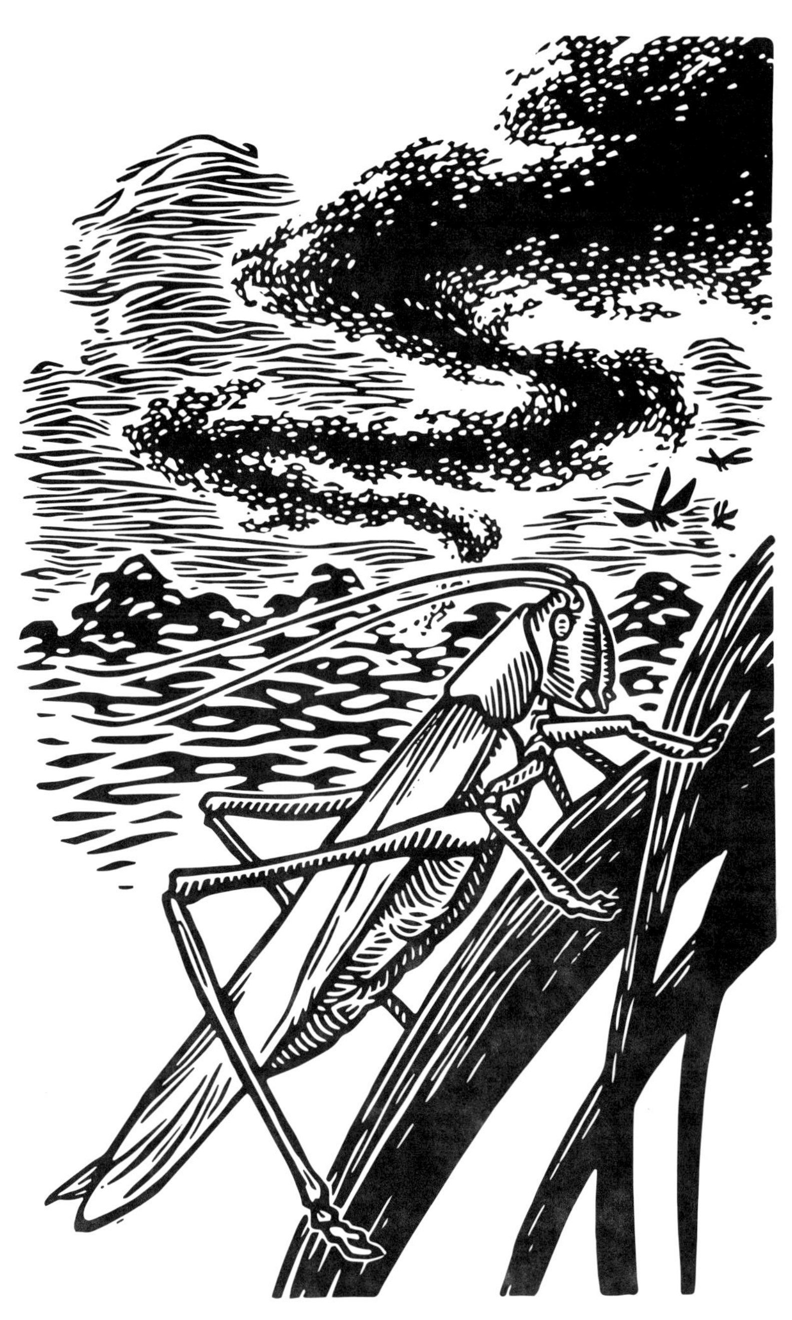

Zombies!

The mush-brained, slack-jawed, decomposing zombie may be the embodiment of soulless modern life, but its origin goes back hundreds of years. In the seventeenth century, France brought enslaved Africans to what is now Haiti. Worked nearly to death, slaves shared tales of a liberated afterlife. Those who took their own lives, however, would be punished by having their souls trapped inside their dead body, forced to work on a plantation for eternity. The legend evolved and has been woven into Haitian Voodoo ceremony, where priests are said to reanimate corpses. Globally, the undead apocalypse has hit the cultural zeitgeist and is ubiquitous in literature, film, and video games.

Could it actually happen? In a way, it already does.

Ophiocordyceps is a parasitic fungus that can infect ants and take over their bodies. The fungus forces the manipulated ant to stumble out of its nest to find an open, humid area. The ant dies and a giant mushroom-like growth erupts from its head. Finally, infectious spores are released upon new unsuspecting victims.

Toxoplasma gondii is a parasite that has evolved to make rats aroused by the smell of cats. The enchanted rat approaches their natural enemy, gets eaten, and the life cycle continues. The parasite continues to pass by contact, even to humans. Millions of people have been infected, but thankfully there have been no human reports of kitten smitten fever. Still, the potential for human brain manipulation is there. Even the normal bacteria in our stomach can affect our mood and behavior. Rabies is a virus that can make humans incredibly aggressive, and just like a fictional zombie virus, is transmissible by bite.

The zombies you see in horror flicks may not be taking over the world any time soon, but extreme evolutionary leaps could theoretically make a virus or parasite strong enough to control the human body. When that day comes, it would be wise to avoid anyone whose head is exploding with mushroom spores.

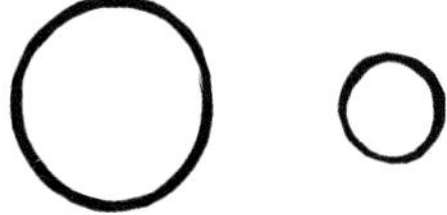

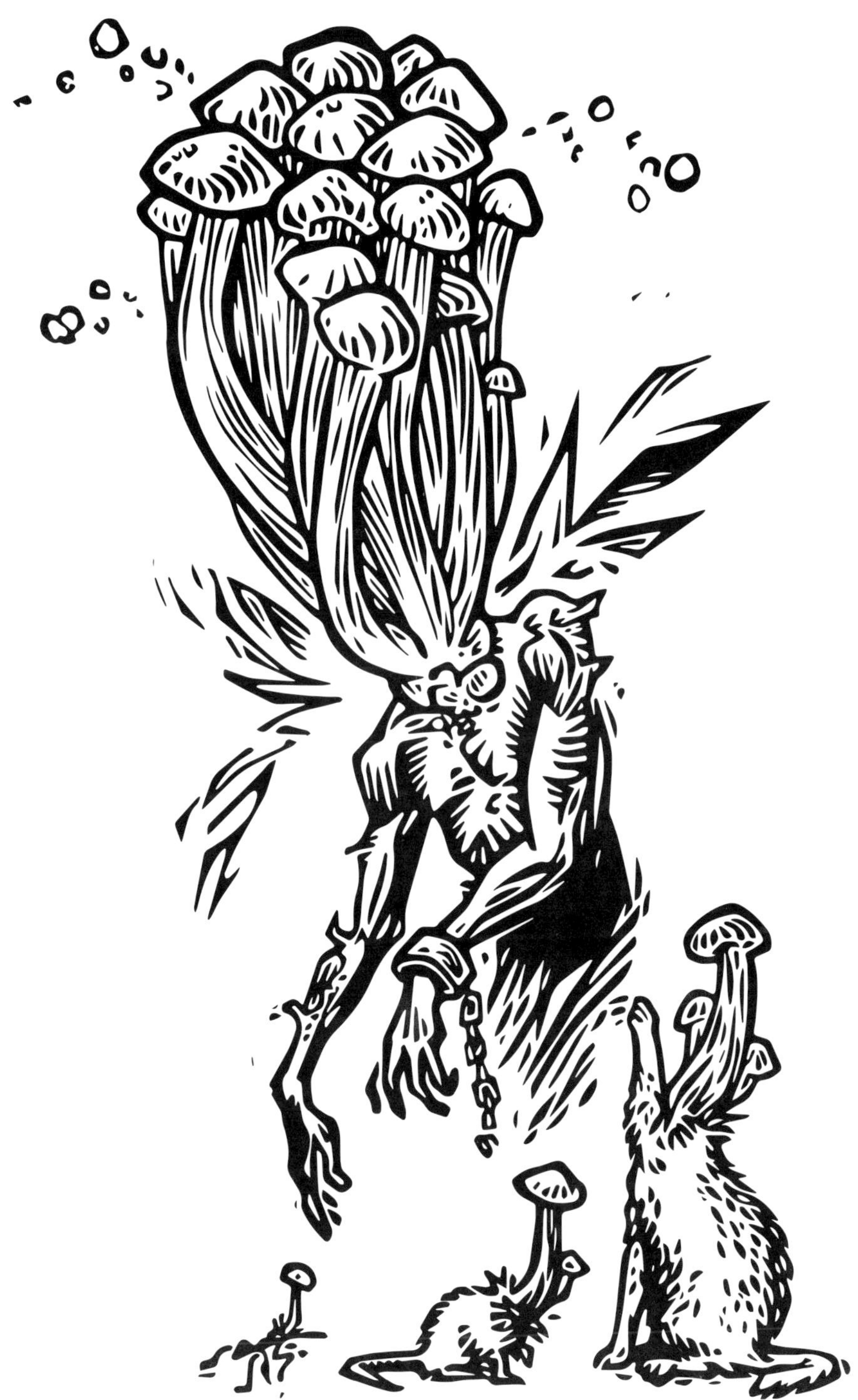

Dark Day

At noon on May 19, 1780, black clouds descended upon New England. American revolutionaries of the time were suddenly enveloped in complete darkness. Candlelight was needed to see anything or walk anywhere. In New Hampshire, where six inches of ash fell from the sky, one resident wrote "A sheet of white paper held within a few inches of the eyes was equally invisible with the blackest velvet." The only evidence of the sun was a tiny glowing red orb hovering in the dark haze.

All spooked inhabitants of the region seemed convinced the world was ending: People sought refuge in churches or taverns, farm animals returned to the barns, and birds sang their evening songs. A Connecticut politician pled to continue delegating, despite the bleak possibilities. He declared, "The day of judgment is either approaching, or it is not. If it is not, there is no cause of an adjournment; if it is, I choose to be found doing my duty." He at least had a new campaign slogan for when the light of day returned. Within a few days, the smoke cleared and normal life of war with the Brits was restored. A year later, grateful observers commemorated the anniversary with fasting and prayer.

Some New Englanders still consider the historical day a fulfillment of biblical prophecy. However, fire-scar evidence has been found in Ontario trees that document a sprawling wildfire dating back to 1780. Smoke from the fire must have drifted hundreds of miles south and combined with heavy fog and cloud covering to create a perfect storm of dusty darkness. It left the region blacked out for days and bewildered for centuries.

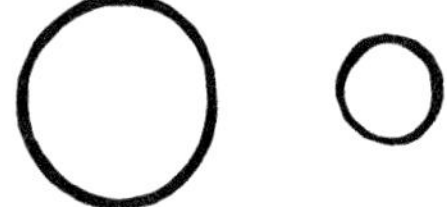

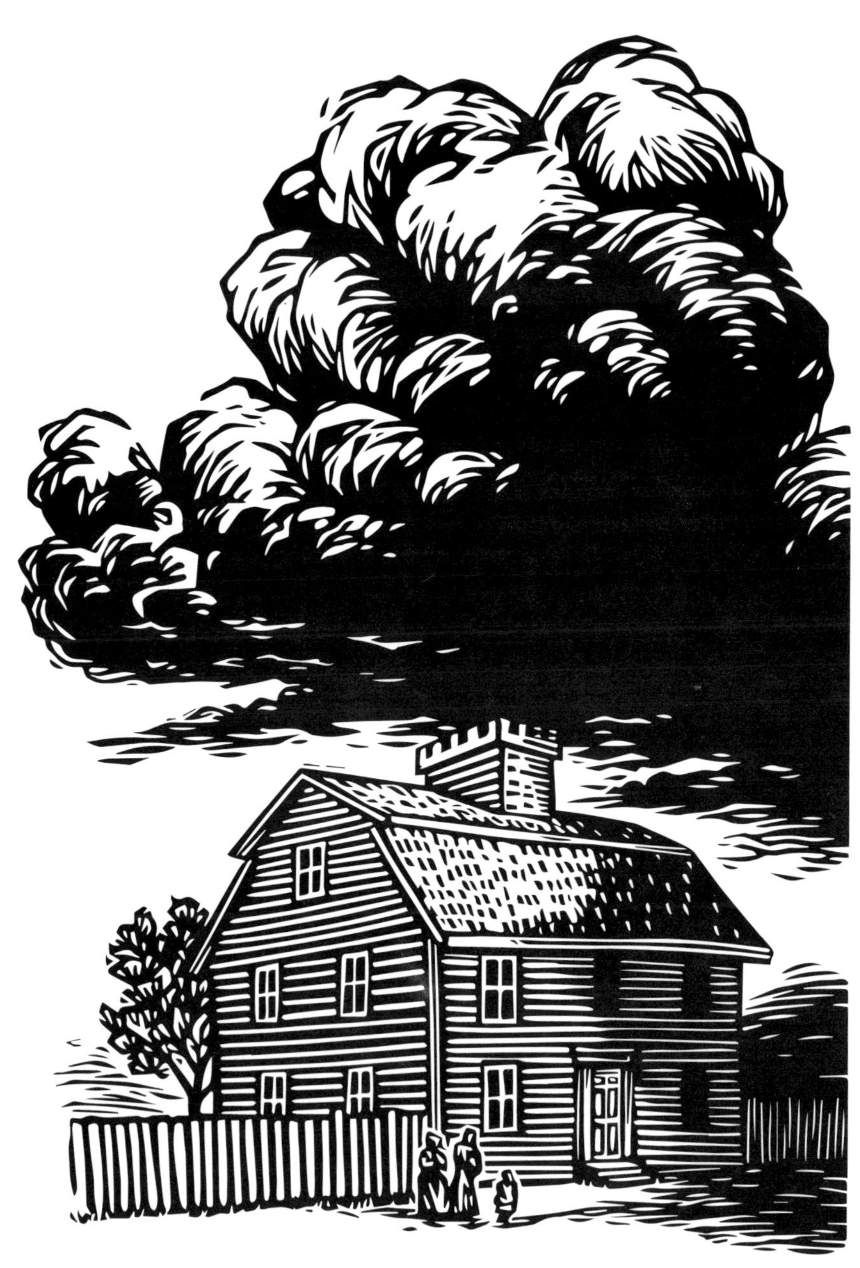

The Prophet Hen of Leeds

Mary Bateman was born in a village near Leeds, England during the Industrial Revolution. It was a prosperous era and people became determined to make money any way they could. The enterprising Bateman made a name for herself as a fortune-teller, miraculous healer, and someone to help ward off evil spirits.

In 1806, Bateman was blessed to have a hen that laid eggs bearing the words "Christ is coming." This declaration is associated with the Judgment Day, so interest was piqued. Every morning, curious locals flocked to view the arrival of these ominous ova, where Mary charged a penny for protection from the nearing end times. However, it was soon discovered that she was etching the phrase onto the eggs and inserting them back into the hen, making the delivery appear natural. Christ was not coming and her reputation was damaged. Soon more revelations were made of her skills as a thief, con artist, and abortionist. She became infamously known as The Yorkshire Witch.

Three years later, Mary Bateman was caught poisoning the pudding of a couple she was defrauding. She was sentenced to death for the murders. Her execution was a public event that lasted three days, including political posturing, hanging, and dissection. Her skin was tanned into leather and sold as magical charms. The city charged three pennies to view her corpse, finding more profit in her infamy than she did with the egg deceit.

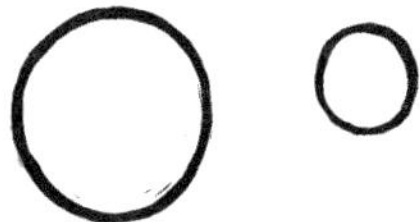

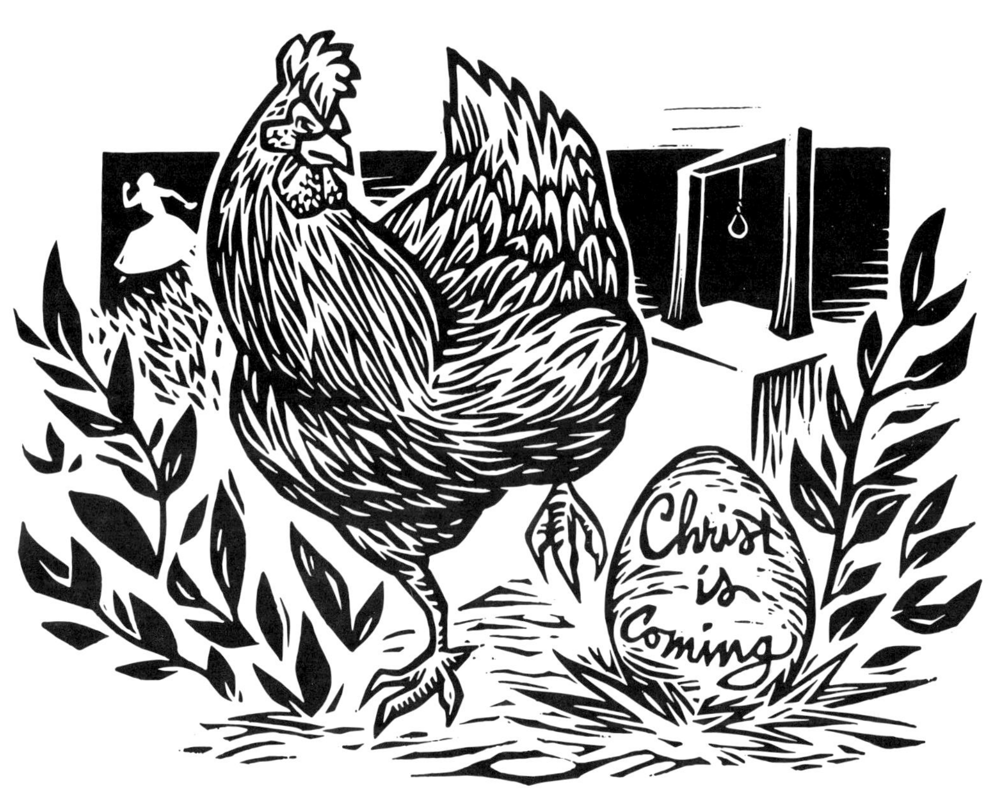

Christ is Coming

Woman of the Apocalypse

At the age of forty-two, Joanna Southcott began to experience apocalyptic dreams and visitations. The former dairy farmer from Devon, England seemed genuinely convinced she had supernatural gifts. Southcott wrote rhyming prophecies and quickly amassed a following of loyal readers. In London, she became the subject of many satirical cartoons and was even mentioned in a Charles Dickens novel. Capitalizing on her fame, she sold exclusive tickets to the 144,000 spots available for eternal life after the Advent.

In 1814, at sixty-four years old, Southcott proclaimed to be a pregnant virgin carrying the new messiah. She named herself the Woman of the Apocalypse, which may sound like your new favorite Avenger but is actually a divine figure from the Bible. Described in the Book of Revelation as a Virgin Mary-like figure, the Woman of the Apocalypse gives birth to the second coming of Christ and ignites Armageddon.

Alas, Southcott's final prophecy would not come true. Instead of spawning a world-crushing baby messiah, she died—likely from a medical condition that caused the abdominal swelling she cited as evidence of her pregnancy. Her devastated supporters refused to believe she was dead and only allowed her burial once the body began to decay.

After her death, a box was discovered that is said to contain prophecies meant to protect the world. She attached a request that it only be opened during a time of great catastrophe, and must be done in the presence of twenty-four bishops from the Church of England. There have been times of national crisis since her death, but no one could gather enough bishops. The box remains in a museum, where modern "Southcottians" protect her wishes and debate its contents. There's still time for this superhero Woman of the Apocalypse to save us yet.

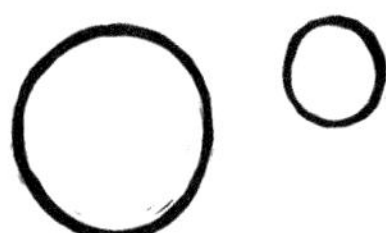

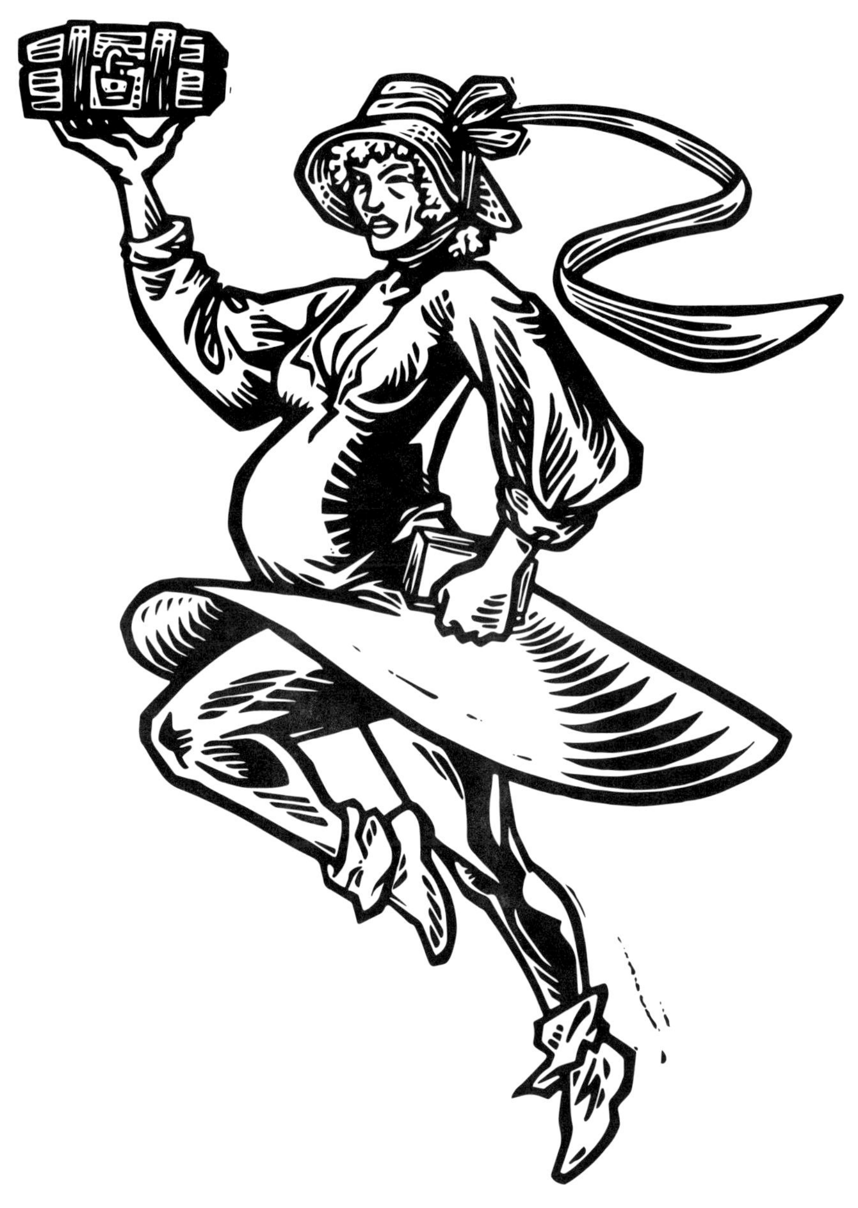

The Year Without Summer

On April 5, 1815, rumbles from Mount Tambora began to reverberate across Indonesia. The volcano erupted continuously for four months—still the largest eruption in recorded history. Nearby homes collapsed under the weight of fallen ash. Ships navigating the surrounding waters struggled through several feet of floating cinders. Volcanic particles drifted into the sky and circled the globe.

Though the immediate effects of the eruption were nightmarish, the worst came the following year. Sulfate lingered in the atmosphere and blocked sunlight. The suffocating blanket of soot caused severe climate abnormalities and agricultural disasters. Summer frost and a loss of sunshine killed crops in North America, Europe, and Asia. Temperatures were erratic, raising to normal levels long enough to give hope for crops, only to drop below freezing and spread despair. Farmers, livestock, and confused migrating birds froze to death in New England, where eighteen inches of snow piled up in June. Parts of America dried up over a 120-day drought, while monsoons drenched China and spread cholera up the River Ganges all the way to Moscow. In Europe, famine brought fears that these dreadful conditions would last forever. People rioted in the streets, unaware that this was a temporary effect of a volcanic eruption a year ago on the other side of the planet.

In a time of adversity comes creativity. As horses starved or were slaughtered for meat, people were forced to look for a new form of transportation. Enter the man-powered Laufmaschine, an early German prototype of the bicycle. Another by-product of the disaster has become a Halloween icon: Mary Shelley's gloomy and bleak summer holiday in Switzerland inspired her to write the horror novel *Frankenstein*. English poet Lord Byron wrote *Darkness*, which encapsulates 1816 by beginning "I had a dream, which was not all a dream. The bright sun was extinguish'd, and the stars did wander darkling in the eternal space."

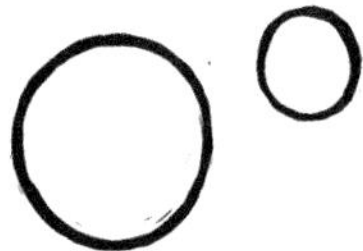

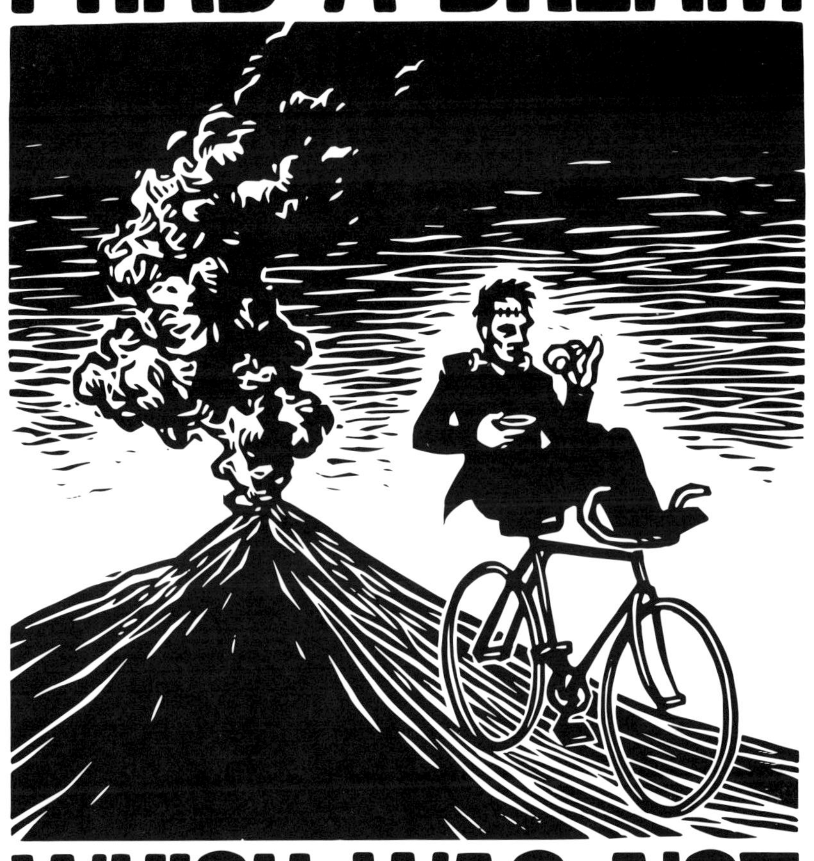

I HAD A DREAM
WHICH WAS NOT
ALL A DREAM

Solar Storms

The Sun has more potential for danger than just giving us squinty eyes and sunburns. The fiery storms that blaze across the surface of the Sun occasionally launch solar flares into outer space. These rays create dazzling displays through the lens of our atmosphere, but also possess powerful electrical currents that could interrupt power lines, electrical grids, and high-voltage transformers around the world.

While most geomagnetic beams zap past Earth, some devastating direct strikes have been recorded. In 1859, a solar flare hit the Northern Hemisphere, filling the sky with aurora borealis lights as far south as the Caribbean. On the ground, the magnetic spectacle wasn't as charming. It sent searing electrical currents racing through telegraph cables, starting fires and injuring bystanders with electrical shocks.

Solar storms that impact us are rare, but scientists estimate a twelve percent chance of one hitting Earth within a decade. Potential damage includes massive blackouts and losing control of fuel and water pumps. Being knocked back into a pre-electrical age would create chaos across the globe, like the dreaded task of having to reset the microwave clock. There are plans to fortify electrical grids with current-blocking devices to protect the technologies at risk, but it remains a hypothetical until needed. When the time comes, you may at least enjoy some mesmerizing magnetic rays at the beach.

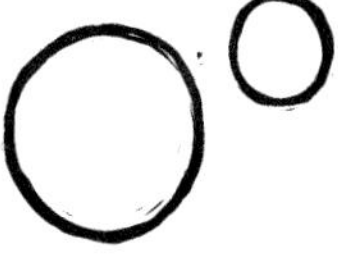

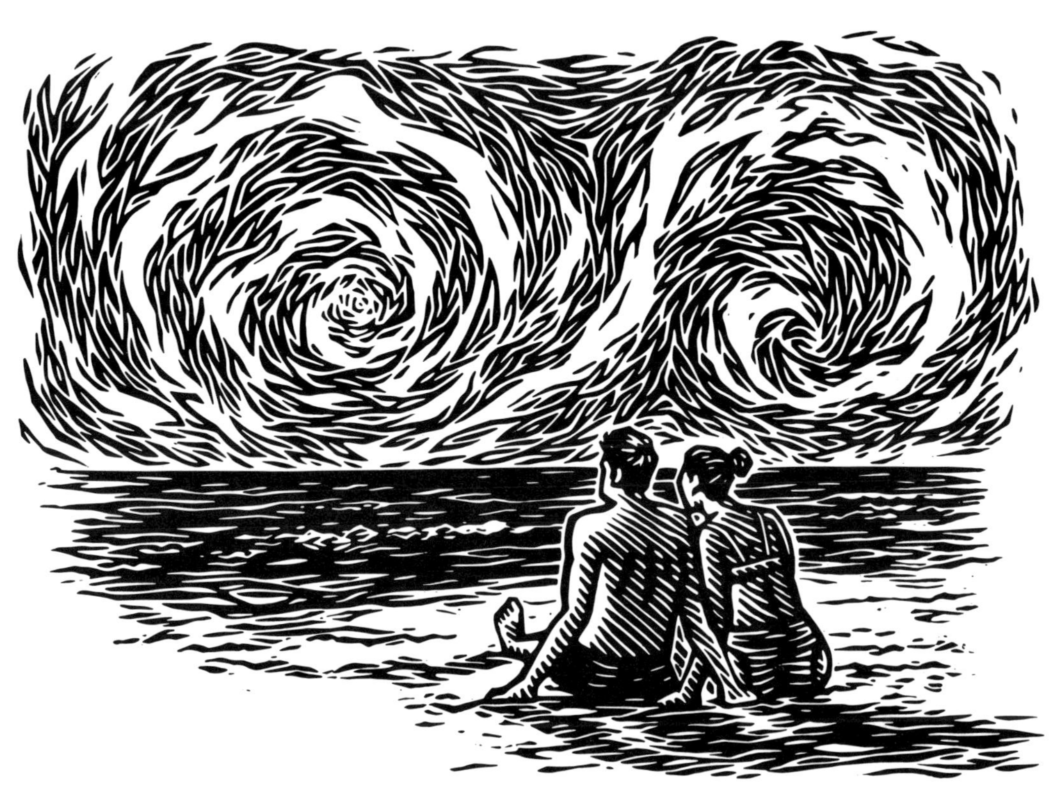

Halley's Comet

In the early twentieth century, people learned that Halley's Comet would soon pass close to Earth, as it does about every seventy-five years. Rumors spread of its powers. Could this celestial mystery with the ominous tail be responsible for strange recent events? Conspiracy theorists blamed the comet for the death of England's King Edward VII, flooding in France, and the looming threat of German invasion. The *New York Times* published an announcement from an astronomer declaring that the comet would unceremoniously end life on Earth.

Throughout this wave of hysteria, entrepreneurs got creative. You could gain protection from "The Evil Eye in the Sky" and its poisonous chemtrails by purchasing and wearing a special gas mask. A Haitian Voodoo medicine was branded "An Elixir for Escaping the Wrath of the Heavens." A couple of enterprising capitalists in Texas were arrested for marketing sugar pills as a comet cure-all, only to be released by police when a mob of faithful customers demanded their freedom.

On May 19, 1910, when Halley's Comet crossed the sky, people packed churches and quarantined at home, sealing themselves from the outside air. Some watched from rooftops and were convinced they could smell the sky burning. A California man nailed himself to a cross, and with his one free hand pushed away rescuers trying to deny his rightful martyrdom. Life went on. The comet would return for a viewing in 1986, and, if you're looking forward to another doomsday, will return again in 2061.

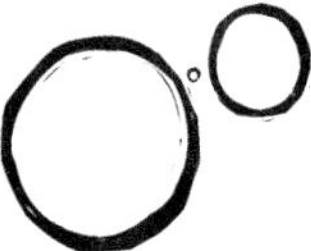

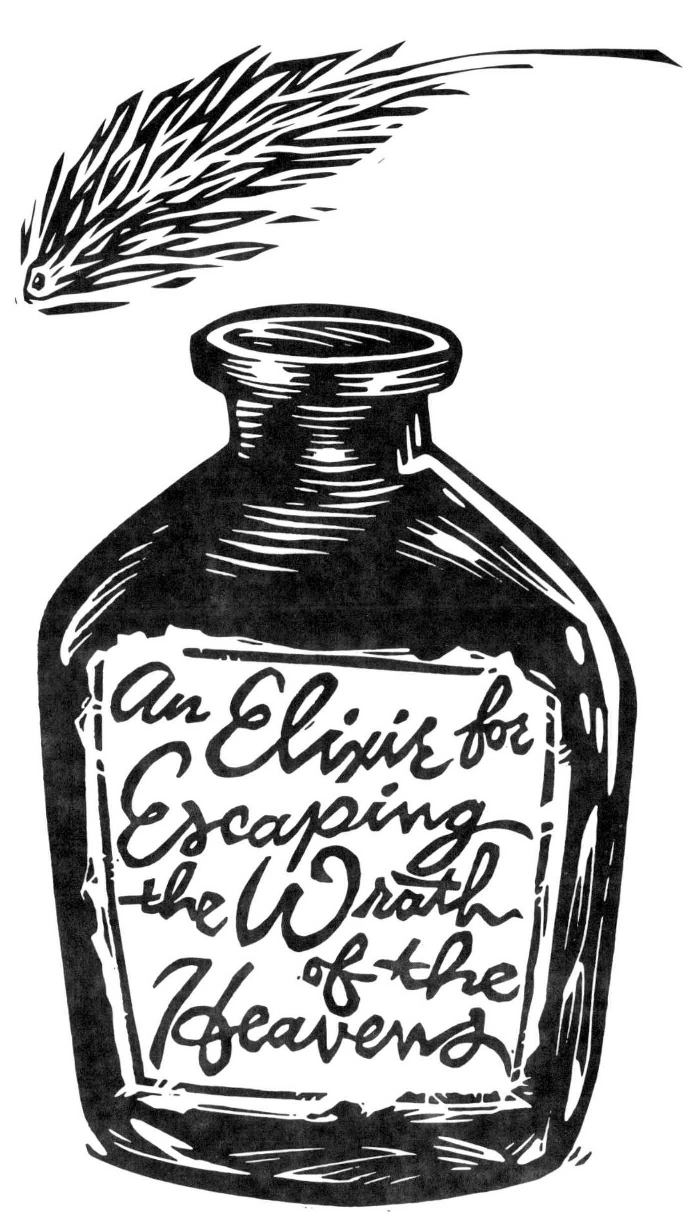
An Elixir for
Escaping
the Wrath
of the
Heavens

Chemical Warfare

Attacking your enemy with toxic chemicals is a battle tactic dating back thousands of years. Ancient fighters would slather blades and arrow tips with filth to inflict extra damage by infection. Armies contaminated water supplies to weaken the opponent before battle. In an attempt to take land without fighting for it, colonizers gave blankets infected with smallpox to natives. And so it goes.

Chemical warfare reached a deadly efficiency in the First World War. Noxious gases were released during battle, engulfing troops in a burning fog. It was an agonizing death for countless soldiers, and many that survived were severely disfigured. The magnitude of casualties and public revulsion led to a global agreement to limit the use of poison in war.

The prohibition on deadly toxins would not last. Agent Orange was used heavily in the Vietnam War to intentionally pollute the environment and render it uninhabitable. It was so effective that it consequentially harmed the health of soldiers on both sides, as well as generations of innocent civilians. More recently, the Syrian government was found responsible for deadly chemical attacks on citizens to suppress political resistance. Tear gas is regularly used by police around the world to shut down protests.

Contaminated air and water may devastate regions for decades, but the biggest threat in chemical warfare today comes from synthetic biology. Governments are developing lethal and highly contagious pathogens that could easily devastate the entire world. Whether a superbug makes it out of the lab by simple human error or is deliberately harnessed by a terrorist organization, the ramifications would be equally catastrophic. The recent coronavirus pandemic has been blamed as such a leak, though unconfirmed. The whole truth is unknown, but it is clear that a more dangerous microbe could arrive at any time.

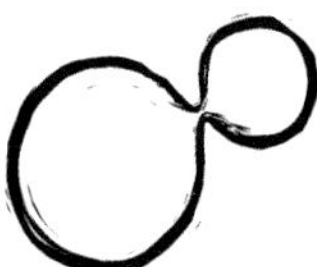

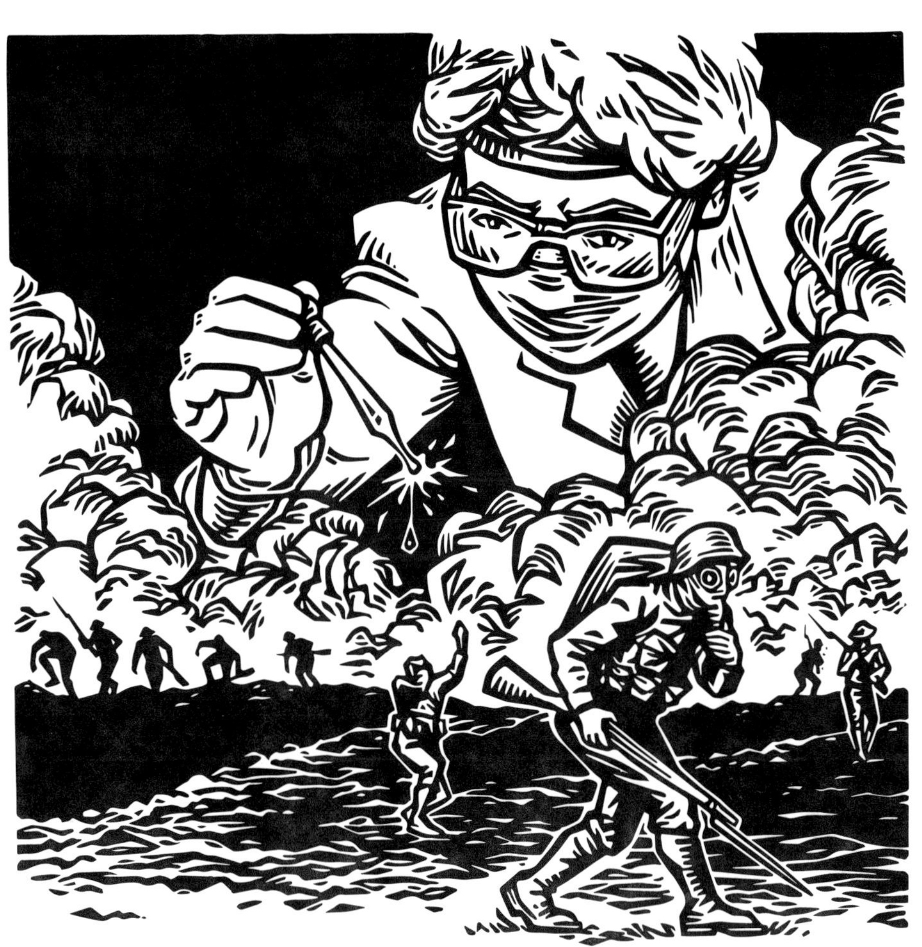

Fire and Ice

Some say the world will end in fire,
Some say in ice.
From what I've tasted of desire
I hold with those who favor fire.
But if it had to perish twice,
I think I know enough of hate
To say that for destruction ice
Is also great
And would suffice.

It would appear everyone has an opinion about the end of the world, Robert Frost included. His 1920 poem describes his internal debate and the conclusion that fire beats ice in the apocalyptic game of chance. He relates fire to the passionate behaviors associated with desire. Perhaps it's our unquenchable hunger that will do us in, like when a totalitarian ruler is controlled by fire and lusts to conquer the world.

Frost then compares ice to the cold-blooded actions brought on by hate, and decides that it too is destructive enough to end the world. Our contempt for each other mounts fear and makes us lash out. It's the ice that compels us to attack a totalitarian ruler that we're convinced is trying to conquer the world. War begins, death spreads, and the world ends. We have two conflicting voices on our shoulders, and whichever wins may determine our peril.

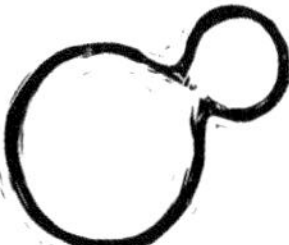

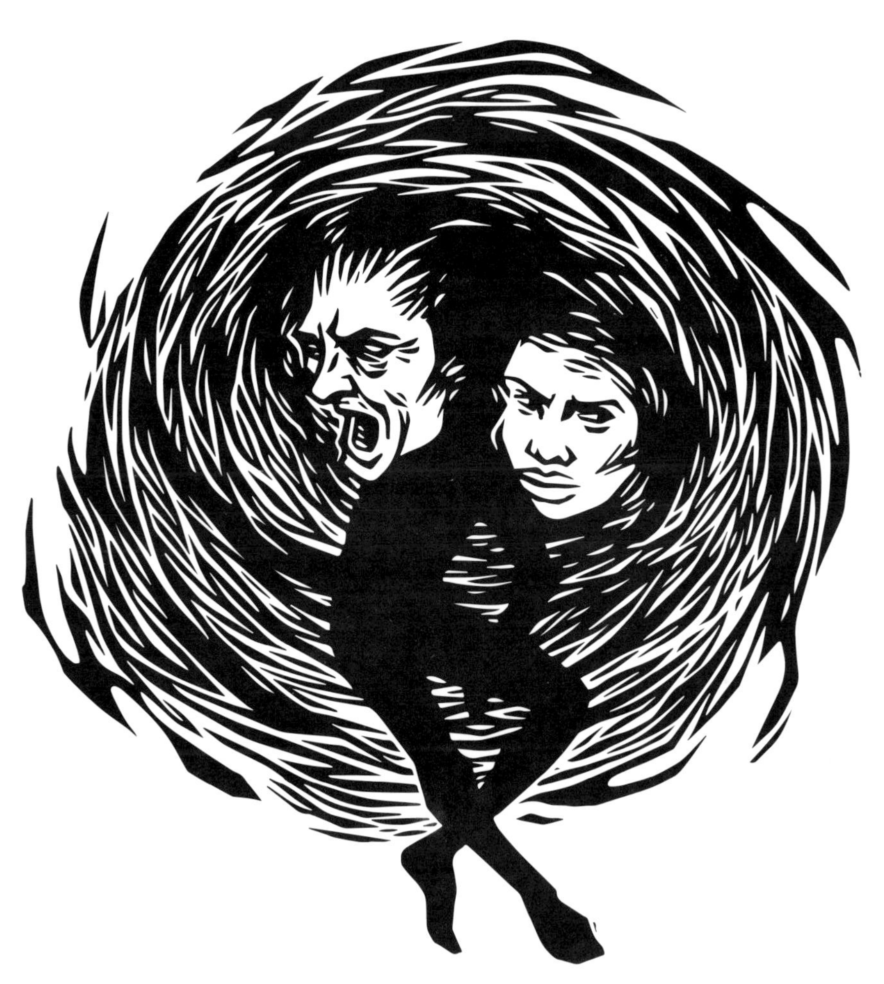

The Hollow Men

This is the way the world ends
This is the way the world ends
This is the way the world ends
Not with a bang but a whimper.

Like Robert Frost, T.S. Eliot was concerned with our downfall and decided there are two options. Eliot wrote these lines to end his poem *The Hollow Men* in 1925, while humanity was still reeling from the Spanish Flu pandemic and the atrocities of World War I. It's reasonable to contemplate existence during a time of senseless and pervasive death.

The dispassionate "hollow men" conjured up earlier in the poem may be a criticism of a rapidly modernizing world devoid of connection and meaning. Our values slip away gradually, unnoticed, until we no longer live in a functioning society. It's like flying a kite at sundown. We let out some thread, it seems to be going well, so we let out some more. The sky is getting dark but it's worked for us this long, so what's a little more? Soon we can't see the kite and we can't feel the string. We don't know when we lost it but it's gone.

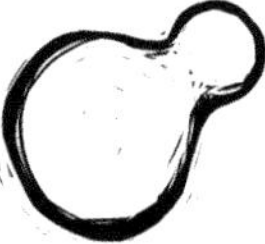

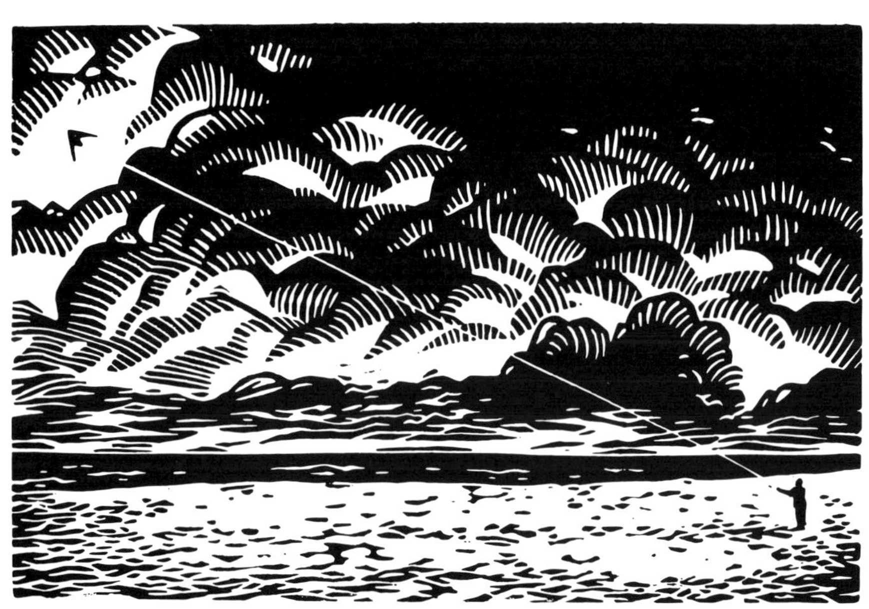

Alien Invasion

We look up at the stars and want to talk to them. Maybe they're just like us. Many tales have been imagined of intelligent extraterrestrial beings coming to Earth to eradicate humans. We're naturally wary of newcomers in general, so it's scary to think that we could be treated the way animals get treated by us. It's fair to assume we would not be able to physically or mentally rival an alien species capable of traveling all the way to our humble planet. Human progress has been impressive, but our own planet is full of reminders that we have room to improve. Our understanding of science still can't produce chemicals as well as plants do naturally. We can't regenerate limbs like salamanders, we're not as athletic as horses, and our emotional intelligence is primitive by elephant standards. Our attempt to understand highly evolved species would be like a chimp trying to comprehend us talking about dinner plans. We're worlds apart and wouldn't have a chance with or against them.

The closest we've ever publicly come to an alien invasion was in 1938. The classic H.G. Wells novel *War of the Worlds* was read over the radio to millions of Americans, with a twist that the story was adapted to be read as a breaking news bulletin describing a Martian invasion in New Jersey. An estimated one in twelve listeners fell for the hoax, creating a nationwide hysteria. There were calls to police, anxious drives out to the country, and unconfirmed reports of suicide. Immense public outcry caused distrust toward news outlets and a tightening of media regulations. The producers of the drama saw the victims as gullible fools.

We don't have any defense against aliens if they're determined to attack us, but that might not be an issue anyway. Astrophysicist Neil deGrasse Tyson has said, "Maybe our biggest protection against being killed by alien civilizations is their conclusion there's no intelligent civilization on Earth."

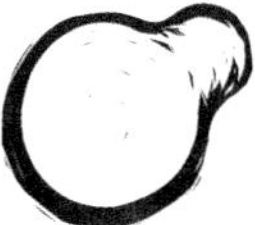

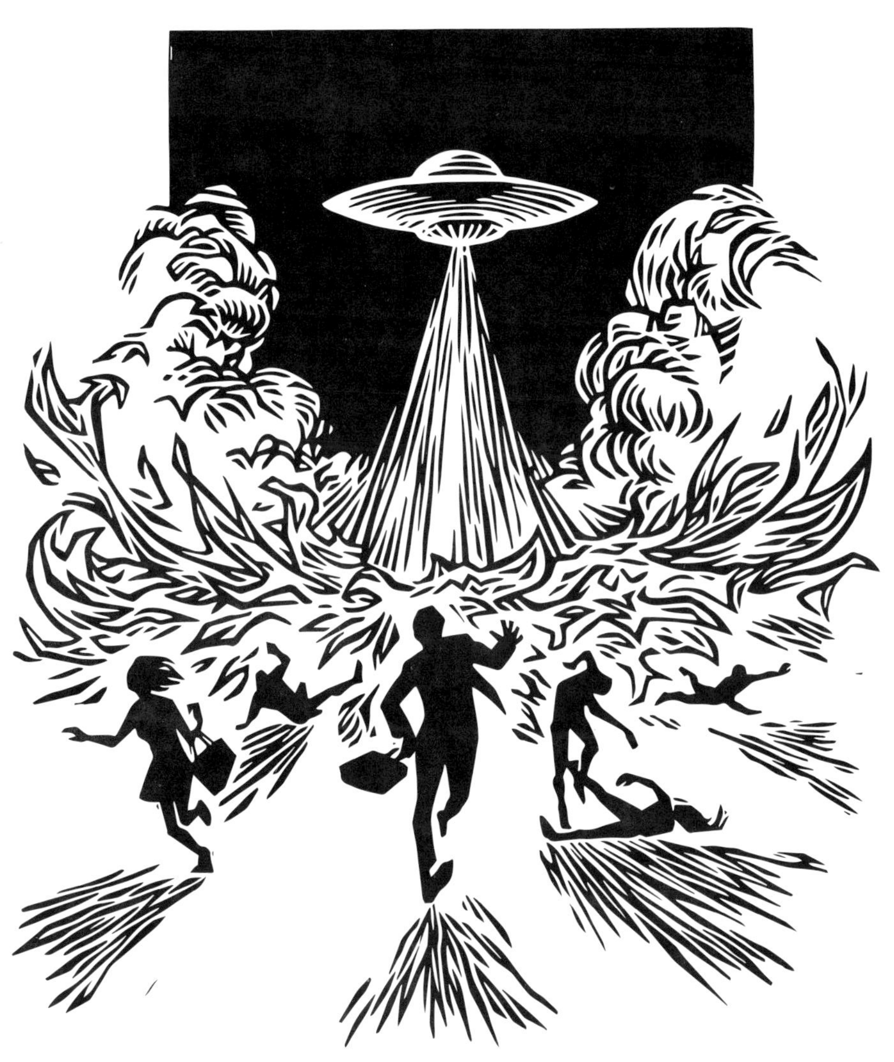

The Sky is Falling

"The sky is falling! The sky is falling!" This is a common idiom used to mock hysteria, usually over a misperception that the world is ending. It originated as an Indian folktale first documented twenty-five centuries ago, but the story has been modified in various cultures throughout history.

In the Brothers Grimm version from Europe, Henny Penny is a timid chick that gets startled by an acorn dropped on its head. Convinced that the sky is crumbling and has knocked its noggin, the only conclusion is that the end is near. The chicken alerts all the animals of the woods about the imminent disaster. The frightened animals come across a cunning fox who tells them it's too dangerous to be outside and promises them safety in its lair. The fox gets them home and eats them one by one.

The 1943 Disney film *Chicken Little* was more specific about the dangers of a charismatic leader stoking paranoia and mass hysteria. The overtly anti-Nazi children's cartoon originally introduced the fox character in his cave while reading Hitler's *Mein Kampf*. The fox devours the animals and with an evil smirk reminds the audience not to believe everything you're told. It was a direct warning to the world.

Some may prefer the Tibetan version, which has a more uplifting ending. Here, the animals meet a brave lion who leads them back to the source of the disturbance, showing them there was nothing to be afraid of. The lion kindly explains to the panicking critters that you must not believe in only words—that it's better to see for yourself.

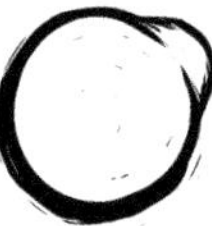

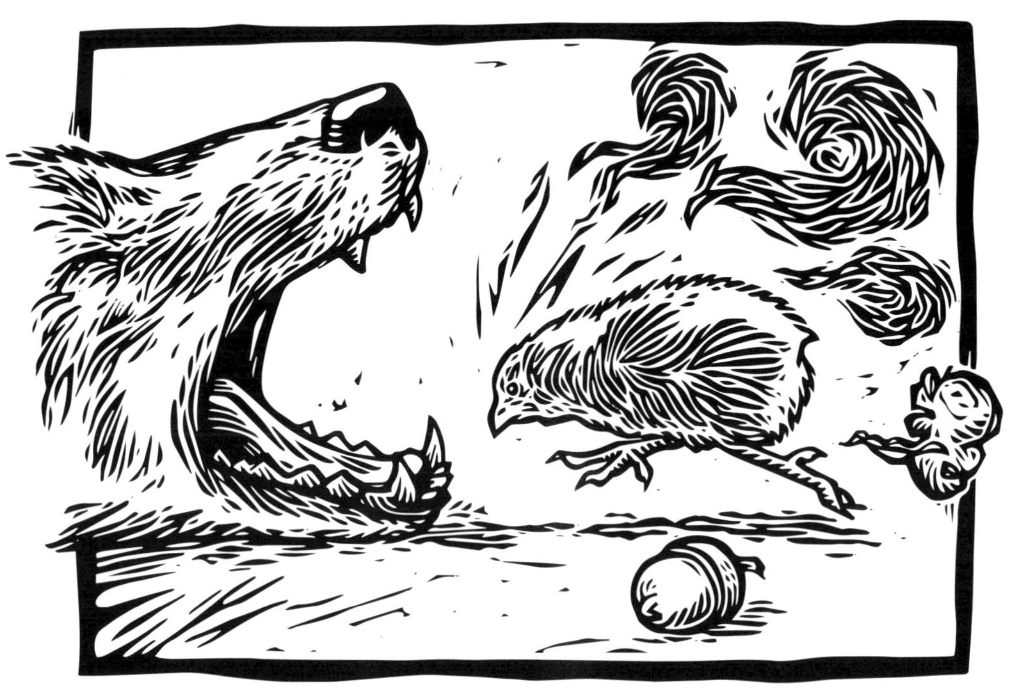

Nuclear Holocaust

World War II set off a race to develop atomic warheads, culminating in the United States dropping two nuclear bombs on Japan in 1945. About 210,000 civilians died in the blasts, forever changing conversations about how wars are fought and the responsibility that comes with weapons of mass destruction.

Battles are traditionally won or lost by the tally of human casualties. After the invention of the atom bomb, the push of a button could instantly decide a victory, thus complicating what it means to win. A superpower could obliterate a smaller unarmed country, or instigate another superpower to push *their* button. Today, acts of aggression between powerful countries are mostly conducted with data hacks and sanctions, but the Bomb remains an option.

With the development of bombs over a thousand times more powerful than those used in 1945, there is a risk of rising geopolitical tensions leading to an escalation of attacks. In this scenario, shock waves circle the globe multiple times while mushroom clouds climb higher into the atmosphere than planes can fly. Smoke from charred cities blankets the sky and blocks out sunlight. Crops fail, ecosystems are decimated, and the oceans' chemistry is drastically altered.

These consequences are similar to volcanic eruptions found in nature, and that's by design. Atomic bombs are unnatural as a product of man-made invention, while being a natural manifestation of human behavior. Nuclear holocaust is the most shameful of our potential outcomes, because it's an extreme result of our worst human traits—hatred, selfishness, and fear.

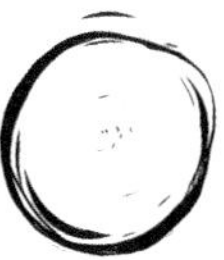

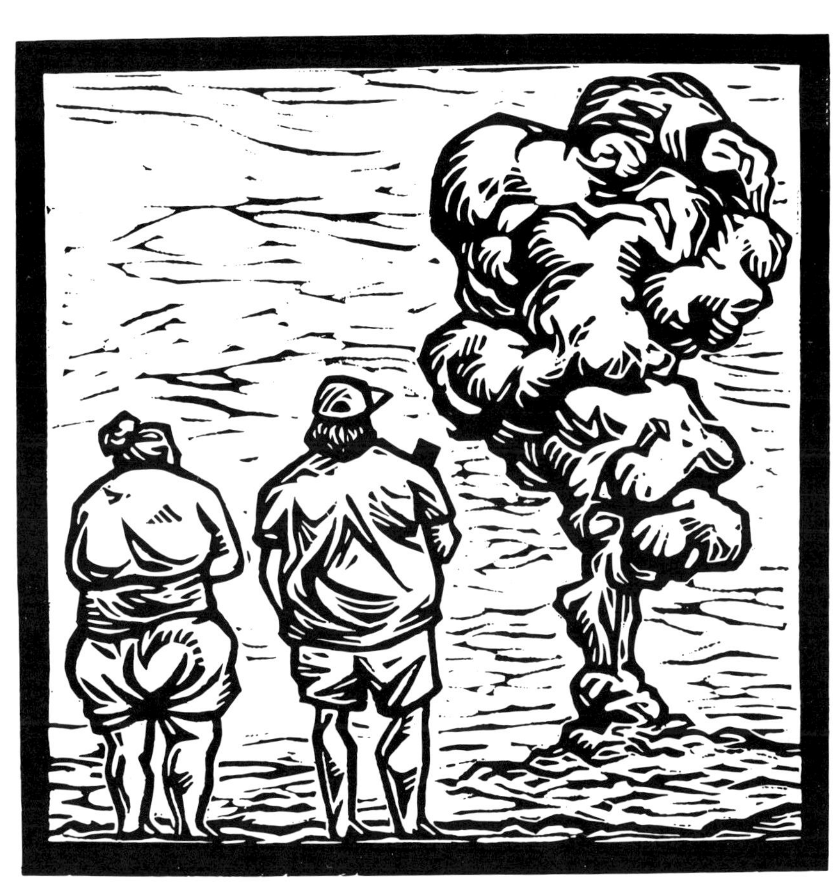

Doomsday Clock

After scientists from the Manhattan Project saw their newly developed atomic bomb used on civilians, they met to discuss its implications for humanity. They determined that people need to be responsible for their inventions, so they organized a Bulletin of Atomic Scientists "to equip the public, policymakers, and scientists with the information needed to reduce man-made threats to our existence."

In 1947, the Bulletin introduced the Doomsday Clock. Though physically located in Chicago, the clock is used as a symbol for how close we are to an apocalypse of our own design. By warning how many metaphorical "minutes to midnight" we have until global catastrophe, it's meant to inform the public and inspire action. A group of eighteen experts in diverse backgrounds meet yearly to decide if the clock's position needs to be changed.

The original setting of the clock was seven minutes to midnight, with nuclear warfare posing the greatest threat. The furthest setting from midnight was seventeen minutes, after treaties were signed in 1991 to reduce nuclear arms. In 2020, the Doomsday Clock moved closer than ever at one hundred seconds to midnight. Experts pointed to nations undermining nuclear arms treaties, a growing climate emergency, information warfare facilitated by the internet, and biosecurity. The Bulletin has warned that these threats have "the potential to destroy civilization and render the Earth largely uninhabitable by human beings."

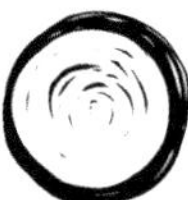

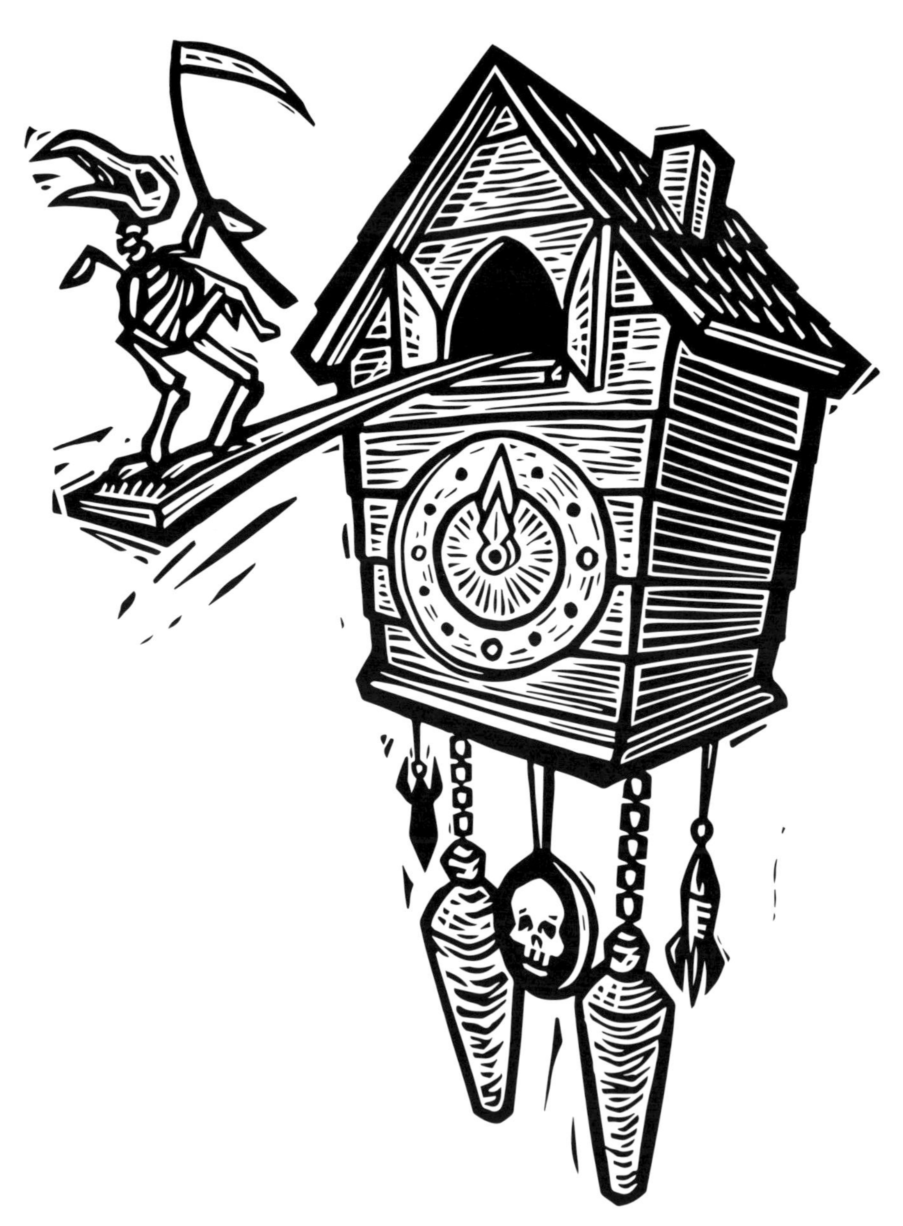

Hopi Mythology

In the years following World War II, religious leaders of the Native American Hopi tribe in Arizona were convinced that the last days of civilization were approaching. Having foreseen a "gourd of ashes" before the bombings in Japan, they decided to share the tribe's secret prophecies with the world. These warnings are said to have been passed down for generations, but without any written proof, they may merely be colorful hindsights of American history.

The first sign of the apocalypse was the arrival of white-skinned men to take the land, "striking enemies with thunder." This is interpreted as European colonizers armed with guns. Further predictions describe the expansion west and propagation of cattle, then "the land will be crossed by snakes of iron." This is thought to be the development of railroad infrastructure in the 1800s. Then there were visions of an entanglement of "a giant spider's web" across the country, presumably power lines. Next, the land would be covered by "rivers of stone," seen as the formation of paved roads and highways. They also saw a black sea of death, signifying harmful oil spills. The final Hopi vision for the end of the world is that a dwelling in the heavens "shall fall with a great crash. It will appear as a blue star." This predicts a space station crashing to Earth. Shortly after, all ceremonies will cease.

When the Dalai Lama met with Hopi elders in the 1970s, he was critical of the prophecies. He said that promoting belief in an inescapable downfall was dispiriting for people, who would resign themselves to fate and be less inclined to change the world for the better.

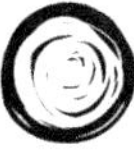

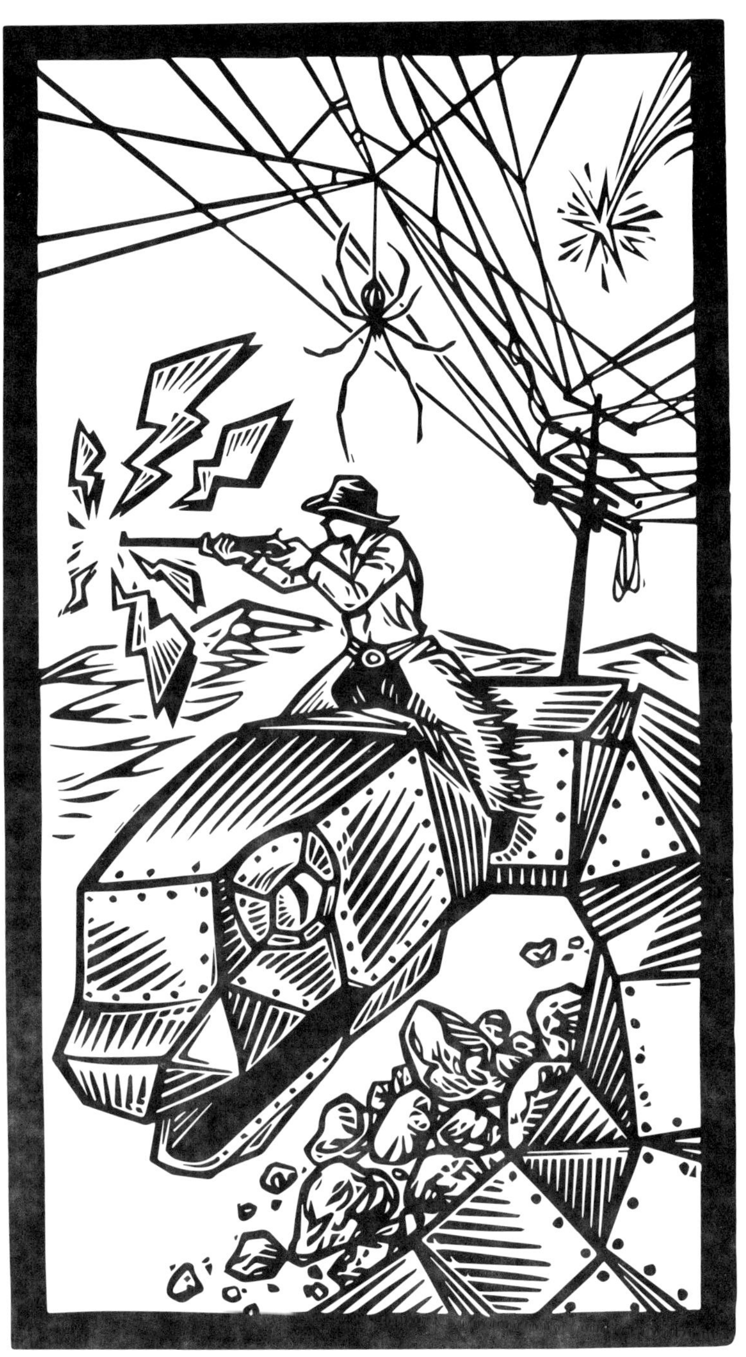

The Cold War

The ebb and flow of tension between the Soviet Union and United States throughout the second half of the twentieth century is known as the Cold War. These global superpowers supported proxy wars all over the world but ultimately made no overt attacks on each other. Ever-growing arsenals of atomic weapons would assure mutual destruction if either side made a move. For those living in the U.S. and Soviet Union at the time, psychological warfare inflicted the worst damage.

Children of the Cold War were taught to "duck and cover" in safety drills at school, though it's still unproven if crouching under a desk would be much help during a nuclear strike. Collective anxiety grew as people searched for ways to protect themselves from the immediate blast as well as the radioactive fog that would permeate the air in the aftermath. Communities designated churches, schools, and libraries as fallout shelters. Families looking for more reliable and exclusive security would convert basements into concrete bunkers. Bonding activities included stocking up on canned corn and telling the kids to stop crying.

Growing up in a world of uncertainty may instill grit and determination to overcome obstacles, or it may burrow into a psyche and create a distrust in society. Today, there are doomsday prepper camps where people meet in the mountains and practice survivalist skills. Old missile silos have been renovated into multimillion-dollar bunkers. Russia and the U.S. still possess 93 percent of the world's nuclear weapons, but children of today aren't trained to fear a nuclear strike. Lessons have been learned and treaties have been signed. Most of the fears of the Cold War generation have been replaced with other heightened anxieties that will shape perspectives of the future.

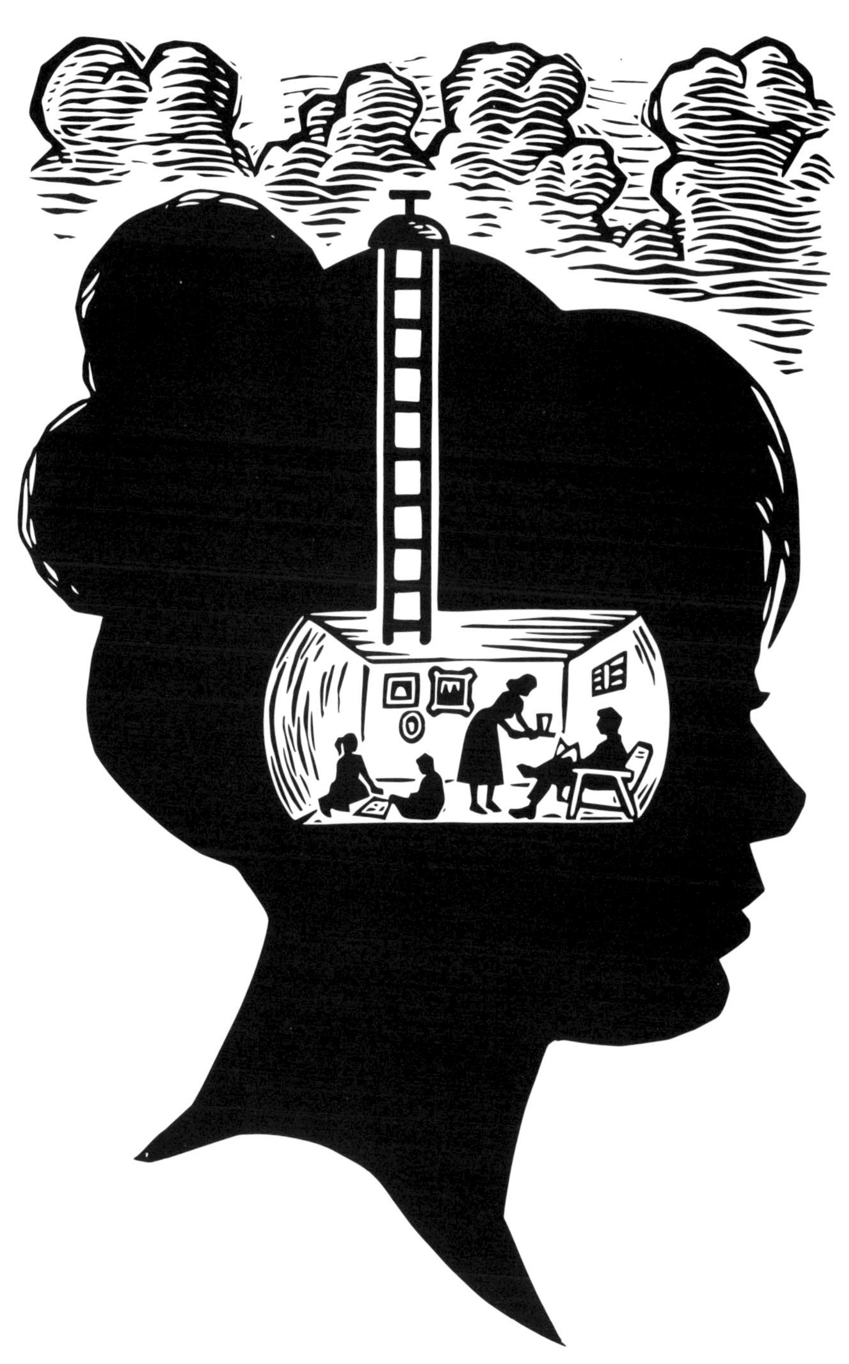

Overpopulation

Rodents have more in common with humans than we'd like to admit. Our physiology and organs are similar enough to make mice ideal test subjects in scientific experiments. Although humans like to be compared to lions and sharks, the alphas of their respective domains, we are probably developmentally closer to scavengers that can adapt and survive harsh conditions. It's the reason humans and rodents have thrived in recent millennia as the two most dominant social animals on Earth.

In the 1960s, people became concerned with overpopulation. Within sixty years, the global population had doubled from 1.5 billion to three billion people. Maryland scientist John B. Calhoun did a series of tests on mice to simulate overpopulation. In Mouse City, a few healthy specimens were placed in a comfortable cage, with ample personal space and unlimited food and water. As the population grew, aggressive males took the dwindling personal spaces, forcing others to fight within the common area. Remarkably, after a certain point in population growth, the fighting stopped. Mice withdrew from interaction with each other. Females stopped making nests to nurture the young. New generations grew up unable to socialize, stopped mating, and the population shrunk. Instead of recovering once the population stabilized, they continued to crowd together for food and water, despite now having plenty of space. The society completely collapsed and all the mice died out. This pathological togetherness to the point of extinction became known as behavioral sink.

Calhoun hoped his experiments would someday lead to finding solutions for stress-related illnesses caused by population density. As our world nears maximum capacity with eight billion people, it might sometimes feel like the dystopian tale of Mouse City. As birthrates drop rapidly, global population is expected to enter a decline soon, which will change how societies function. It's an opportunity to redesign our world to make a healthier and more harmonious environment for all inhabitants.

○

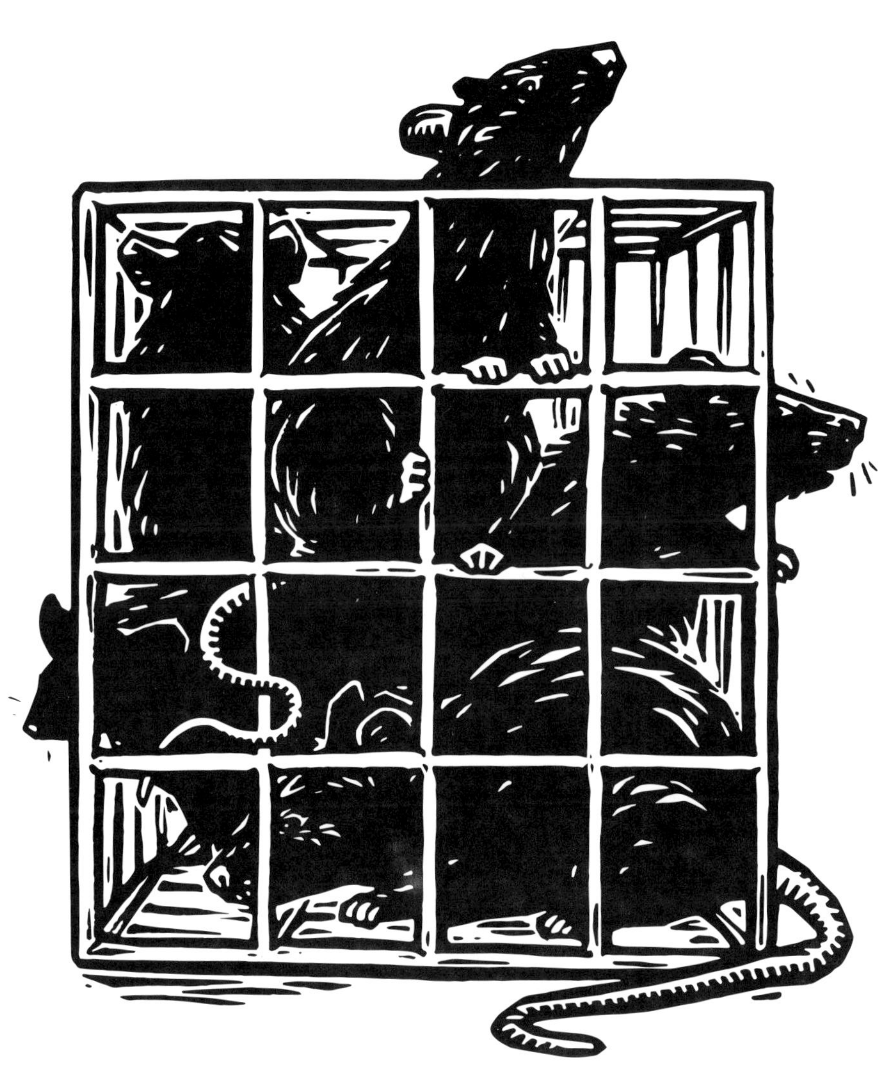

Y2K

As with many diverted disasters, Y2K seems so quaint in hindsight. How could we think a minor computer glitch would destroy the world?

Leading up to the turn of the millennium, there was a global fear that computers would not be able to process the rollover of dates from 1999 to 2000. Digital timestamps were abbreviated to just two digits, with computers programmed to process up to 99 but not 00, so any new data would become invalid on midnight of January 1st, 2000. Due to our growing reliance on computers, theories of worst-case scenarios spread rapidly. The media anticipated power outages, food and gasoline shortages, and financial institution shutdowns. Religious fundamentalist Reverend Jerry Falwell declared the impending crisis would lead to the rapture and advised followers to stock up on guns. A survivalist movement of food hoarding and bunker planning became mainstream, while others dismissed the hullabaloo as a bunch of hogwash. It was a global story that would keep everyone glued to the television on New Year's Eve.

In the end, very few computer failures were reported, leading some to believe that Y2K was never a legitimate concern to begin with. It's possible that disaster was averted by the billions of dollars spent globally in a scramble to reprogram data systems. We'll never know for sure. In any case, it proved to be the first time our own technology showed potential to escape our control. Computers now use dates of four digits instead of two.

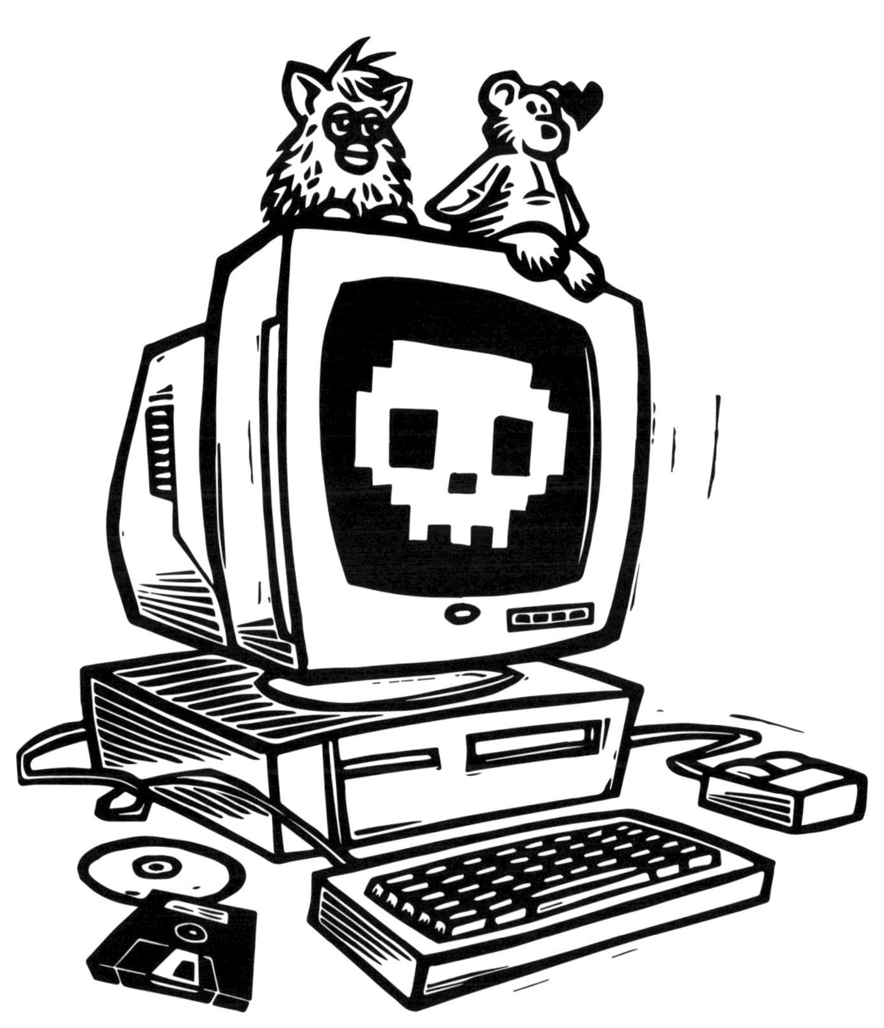

Black Hole

Black holes suck. If we were to approach one in the wild black yonder of space, its gravitational pull would tear us apart with the same force that moves all the oceans on Earth to create tides. Black holes from outer space were formed along with the universe, and thankfully none of the estimated ten million black holes in our galaxy are on a trajectory for Earth. That doesn't mean we're safe. Scientists looking to fill their cosmic void might be making an all-devouring abyss in our own backyard.

In 2008, a Large Hadron Collider was built on the border of Switzerland and France. The massive accelerator shoots subatomic particles at each other in a seventeen-mile-long underground tunnel. It studies kinetic energy on the same extremely high level that once sparked the expansion of the universe. Since this was the first technology of its kind, there were many conspiracies of its potential power. Aside from the obvious fear of it opening a portal for Satan to come finish the job, there were more scientific concerns that couldn't be answered until it was turned on. Since particles colliding have the power to create the universe, people feared that it could also end it.

The particle collider could theoretically produce a black hole, but nothing on a cosmic scale. Black holes range in size from as tiny as an atom* to as large as a billion Suns combined. The collider may be powerful for human technology, but modest by nature's standards. It continues to smash particles and provide valuable information about the existence of our universe, now with confidence that it won't swallow the world.

* Albeit a tiny atom with the same compact mass as a large mountain.

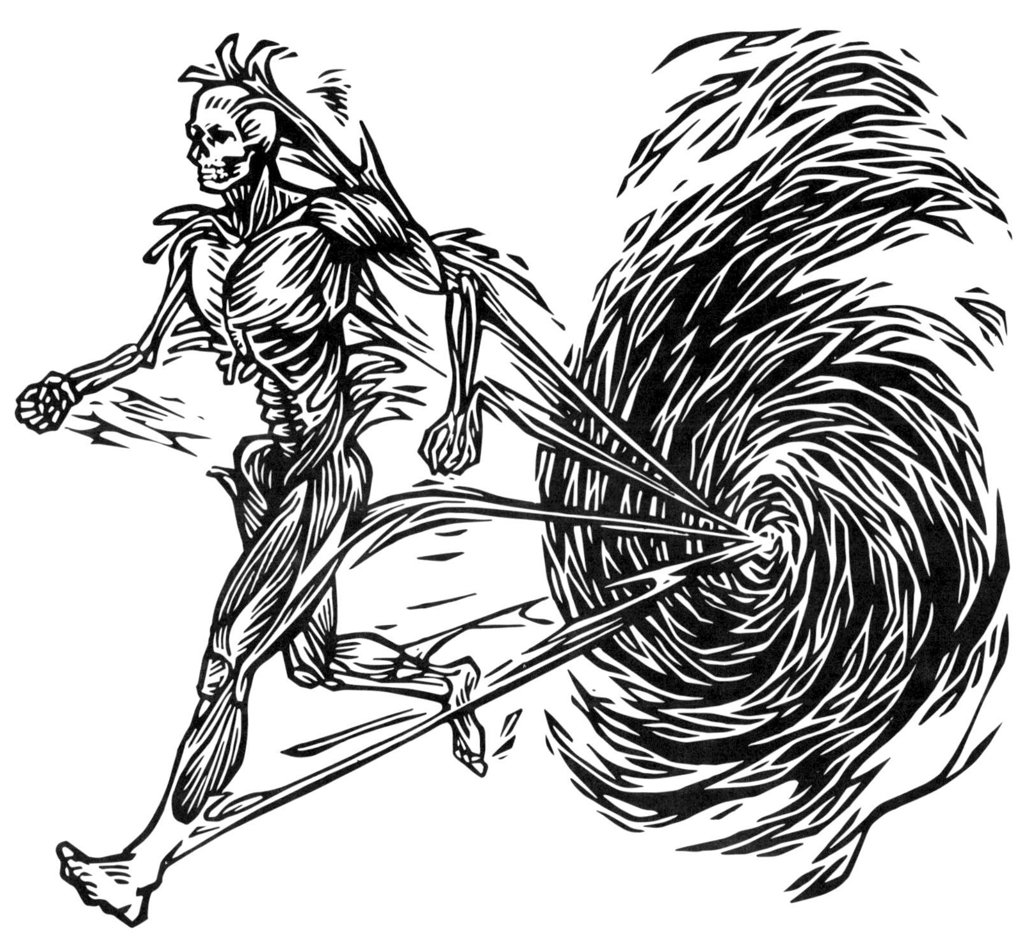

Mayan Calendar

The world did not end on December 21st, 2012. The Earth continued rotating and revolving despite the ancient Mayan calendar ending on that date. There was no collision with another planet, or total blackout, or the world bursting into flames—all of which were theorized by people on the internet. It was just another day full of life and death, which might have been the Mayan prophecy all along.

The Maya were an advanced civilization for their time. Originating in Central America around 2,500 B.C., they developed agriculture, built temples and pyramids, and left hieroglyphic writing to be studied for millennia. They were particularly skilled in mathematics, instituting the concept of zero and accurately determining a solar year. Instead of using this solar cycle to restart the calendar like we do today, Mayans established a long linear calendar that lasts thousands of years. The expansive timetable was scheduled to end in 2012, leaving debate over what would come after. There is a single damaged stone tablet that references the cryptic conclusion, which describes a god's arrival to end the old world and begin the new. However, it lacks a description of what this new world would be. Modern sleuths speculated tirelessly, hoping that our ancient predecessors could provide us with guidance through the uncertainty of the present.

Researchers believe that the Maya had no interest in predicting the end of the world. After all, they had no foresight of the Spanish conquest and the demise of their own civilization. If we want to look for substantial meaning in the calendar ending, it might be that we merely had the lucky timing to be alive through the transition from one Mayan period to the next.

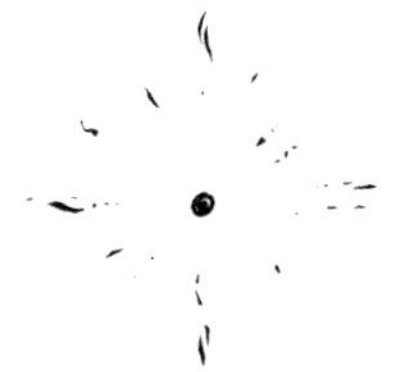

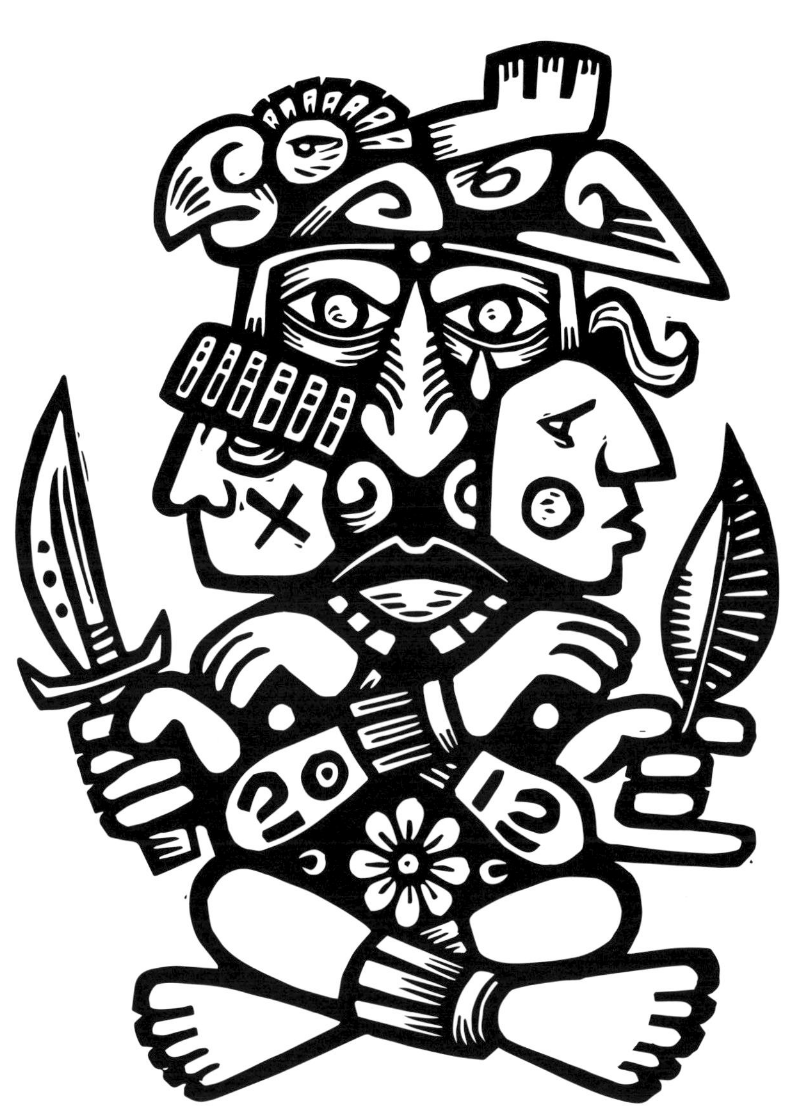

Global Warming

The apocalypse doesn't always happen overnight. There's not a single monumental event to convince us that the climate has changed. Global temperature has been on a gradual climb since the Industrial Revolution, when we discovered our fondness for pollution and deforestation. Many parts of the world are already seeing obvious changes to their way of life. People are now regularly exposed to raging wildfires, intense storms, lethal heatwaves, and rising sea levels. Some climate scientists view these crises collectively as the beginning of a long, drawn-out apocalypse. More of a whimper than a bang.

By the end of this century, nations could be at war over scarce water supplies. Droughts will force mass migrations. The destruction of coastal habitats could leave even superpower nations stretched thin as a tenth of the population would become refugees.

Long-term, birds and reptiles can easily adapt, but mammals and fish will slowly bake and boil along the equator. Just like during the dinosaur times, mammals may be forced to hide from the heat during the day and only come out at night.

Global warming is real and by all scientific reasoning this is not another mistaken doomsayer forecast. We've been daring the teetering sky to fall on us for some time, and now it's here. However, that doesn't mean we're without hope. One lesson to learn from our many brushes with the apocalypse, real or imaginary, is to never underestimate how resourceful humans can be. When under pressure, we have proven ourselves capable of finding a way to survive. The goal now is to minimize the effects of pollution and implement renewable energy on a global scale.

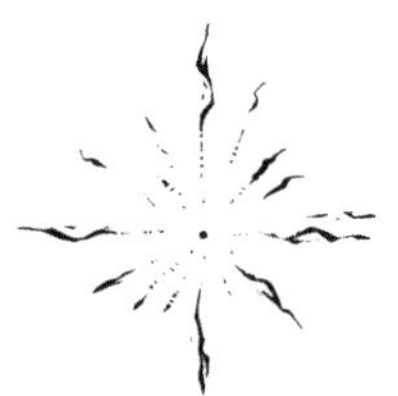

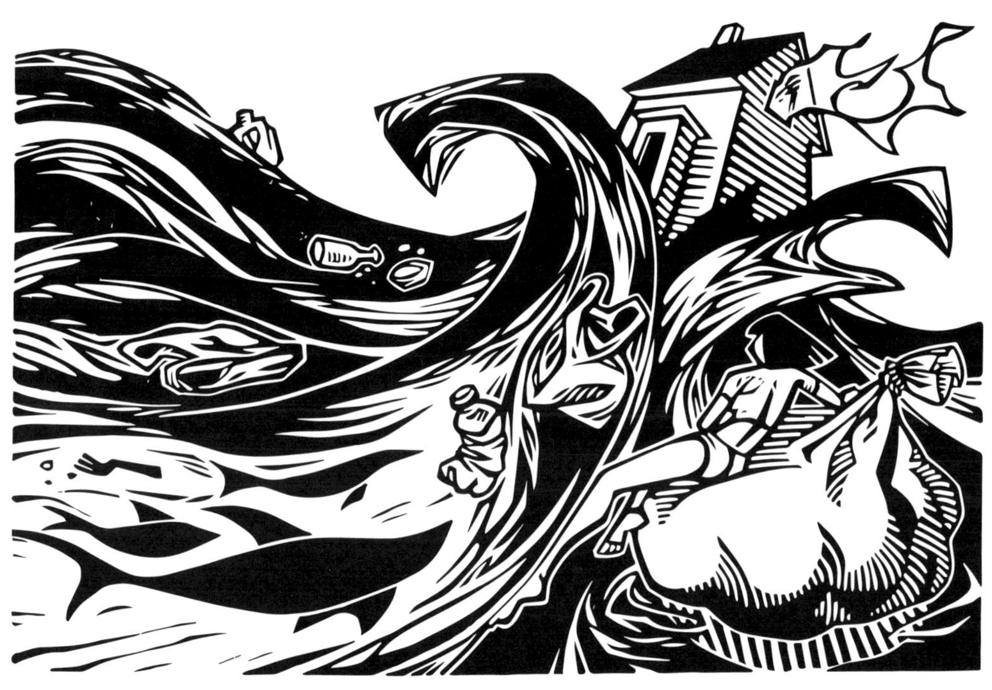

Solar Geoengineering

One proposed solution to climate change may be worse than doing nothing at all. Solar geoengineering is the process of shooting sunlight-reflecting particles into the atmosphere, thus reducing the amount of radiation on Earth and reversing global warming. It's similar to what happens after a volcanic eruption—aerosol particles spread across the globe, blocking some sunlight and temporarily cooling the Earth. If we could harness that power and apply it with pinpoint precision, we can continue pumping greenhouse gases into the atmosphere with no concern. It has potential to be a quick and inexpensive solution to one of the world's biggest threats. Harvard University is currently running field tests to explore geoengineering techniques called "sun dimming," while media outlets and high-profile figures like Bill Gates hail it as an answer to our problems—which it may in part be.

However, sun dimming on a global scale has never actually been tried before. We only get one shot at fixing the problem of climate change, and if we're wrong, it could quite literally mean the end of the world. Solar radiation management could affect weather patterns and increase monsoons in vulnerable parts of the world. The reduced light would have unknown consequences for plants, agriculture, and solar power production. Most importantly, a temperature-modified planet would not prevent the long-term damage of rising carbon dioxide levels caused by pollution. The unflinching fossil fuel economy would remain intact while we continue to spoil the air we breathe and the chemistry of the oceans.

People are drawn to quick fixes enabled by technology and innovation. It's more exciting than acknowledging that we need nonpolluting alternatives to our current industrial systems. Unfortunately, the answer may be more political than technological.

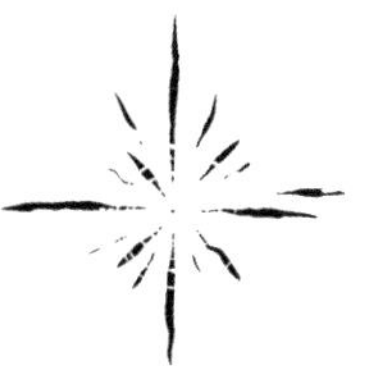

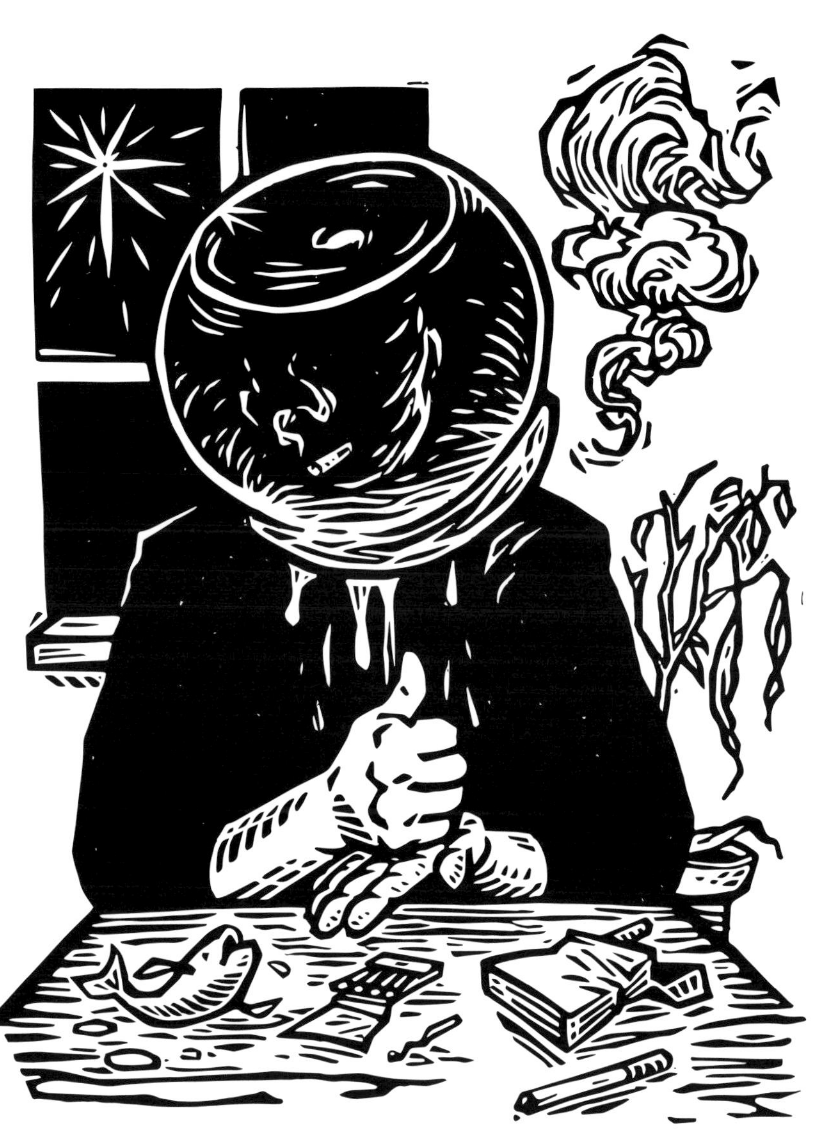

Artificial Intelligence

Our fear of technology supplanting humanity is more than just an action movie trope with cool guys in sunglasses. There are legitimate concerns that reliance on technology could at some point overpower free will in humans. Once computers are programmed to think, learn, and communicate entirely without people, it would make human existence nonessential. We would no longer have control of the system so our own future would be determined by artificial intelligence. Tech businessman Elon Musk believes AI is humanity's biggest existential threat, once comparing computers overtaking mankind to our current relationship to anthills. It would be malicious for us to walk up to an anthill and stomp on it, but we think nothing of wiping out many of these bustling communities whenever we construct a highway. All of humanity may end up being just an anthill in the way of technology's highway.

The benefits of artificial intelligence are clear. Our lives would be easier with computerized manufacturing, agriculture, transportation, and problem-solving. The eventual risks are less obvious. Big Tech algorithms have already proven to shape our thoughts and emotions, but that's just the beginning. There's no current plan to protect ourselves from technology run amok. Could a computer program someday write and illustrate a book about the end of the world? Yes, and it would require less coffee and editing!

The next couple of decades will be crucial for determining how we envision AI supporting humanity. We have forever held the strategy of advancing technology and *then* figuring out how to use it. For AI to be successfully directed, we need preemptive planning to make sure we're not left behind. If all else fails, we can hope to summon a pair of science fiction saviors to protect humanity from our robot overlords.

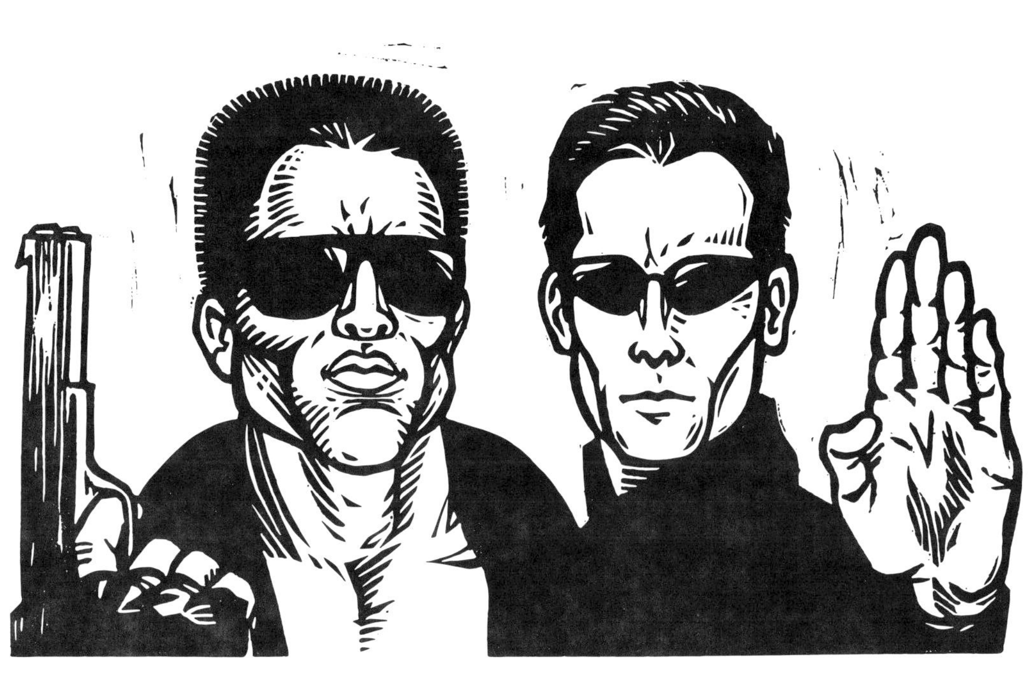

Famine

"Famine" sounds like an Old World problem that wouldn't happen in a modern society full of takeout joints and all-you-can-eat buffets. It's a fear that dates back to tales of the Four Horsemen of the Apocalypse, but the modern iteration predicts the disappearance of more resources than just food. Earth's metabolism is being drained of nourishment in water, land, and air.

Humans are overfishing the oceans, which disrupts the food chain and ecosystems of the water. On land, we're running out of farm space and depleting the finite phosphorous that plants need in soil. Underground fossil fuels are being extracted at a rate that will run out within a lifetime. The atmosphere is being pumped with the gas by-product of those fossil fuels, leaving cities stricken with skidmark skies. According to sustainability experts, we currently need 1.7 planets to support humanity's demand on Earth's ecosystems.

If we can't respond quickly enough by committing to renewable energy, a backup plan may be needed sooner rather than later. Once Earth's resources are depleted, we could colonize space and begin a new chapter of human existence. The possibility has become more realistic with recent developments in rocket design, astrophysics, robotics, and 3D printing. However, it won't be an easy transition for the first pioneers. Space colonists would face deadly radiation, cramped living spaces with low gravity, and the psychological toll of being removed from society. It would be a big advancement for mankind, but hopefully not a step made in urgency due to the destruction of our home planet.

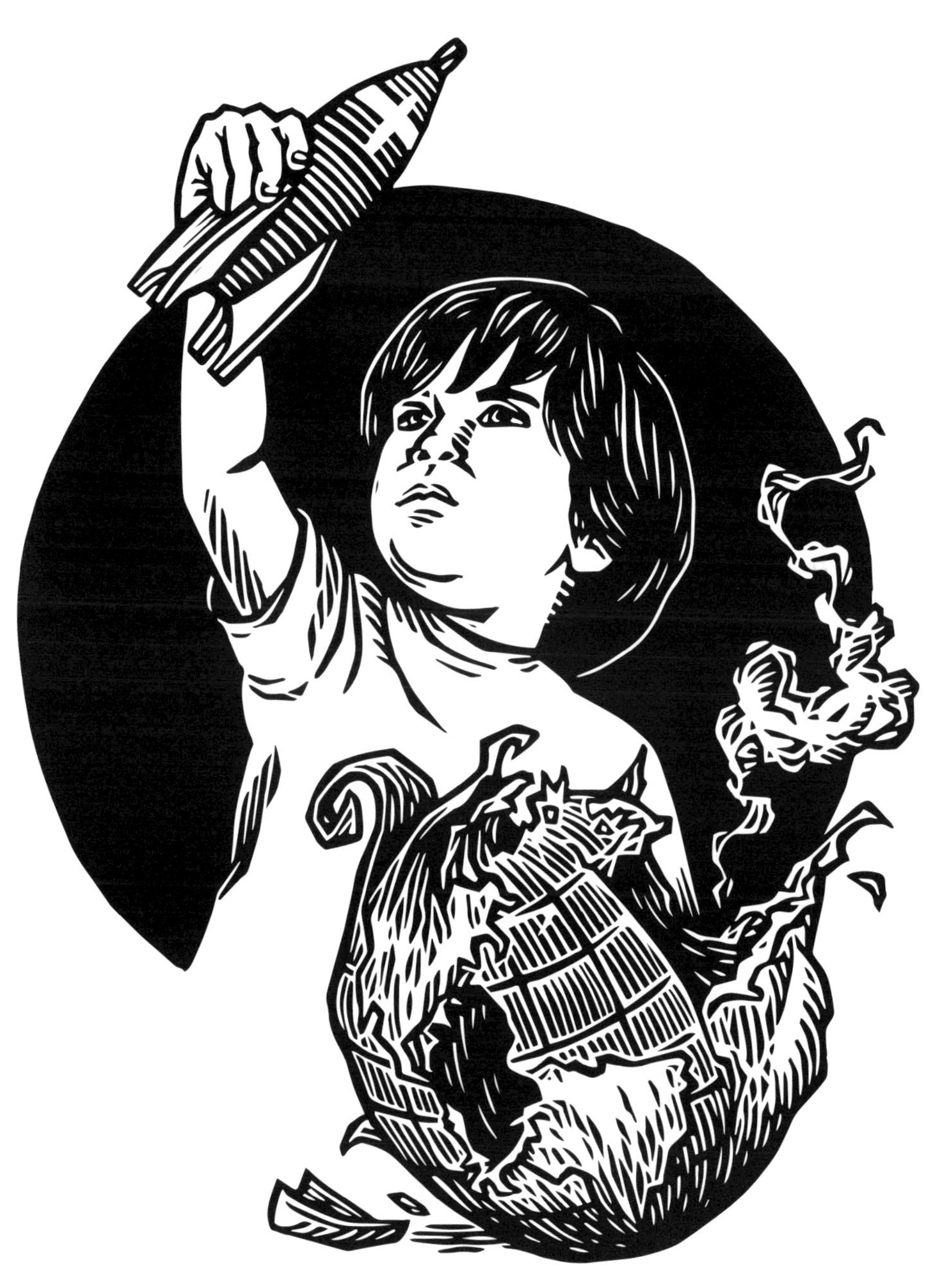

Sun Inflation

If Earth survives all of the damage inflicted on it over the next few billion years, the final boss battle is with an angry Sun trying to devour us all. It's a healthy and happy middle-aged star today, but when its long lifespan comes to a close, it will take our solar system with it.

In this fateful scenario, our friendly reliable source of nourishment in the sky begins to swell. It shines so bright that it boils Earth's oceans, leaving our dry and withered remains to drift through space, defeated and longing for the good old days of life on Earth. The sun has exhausted the last of its fiery yellow hydrogen power, and it grows into an unrecognizable red giant of flaming helium gas. Blinding rays of light stretch far across the solar system, vaporizing every atom along the way. Once all nuclear energy reserves are depleted, there will be nothing left but a glowing white ball of dust.

This is all expected to happen in the very distant future. If humans still exist, then we will have already moved into space and would now need to vacate the galaxy. We'll need DNA printers capable of producing the essentials for life without a home. Species would be protected and transported by storing genetic blueprints in a way that does not require physical bodies. Not a single human form will be present for the preservation and sharing of our kind. It would require a reliance on artificial intelligence to locate another home light-years away, where we can settle and restart our existence.

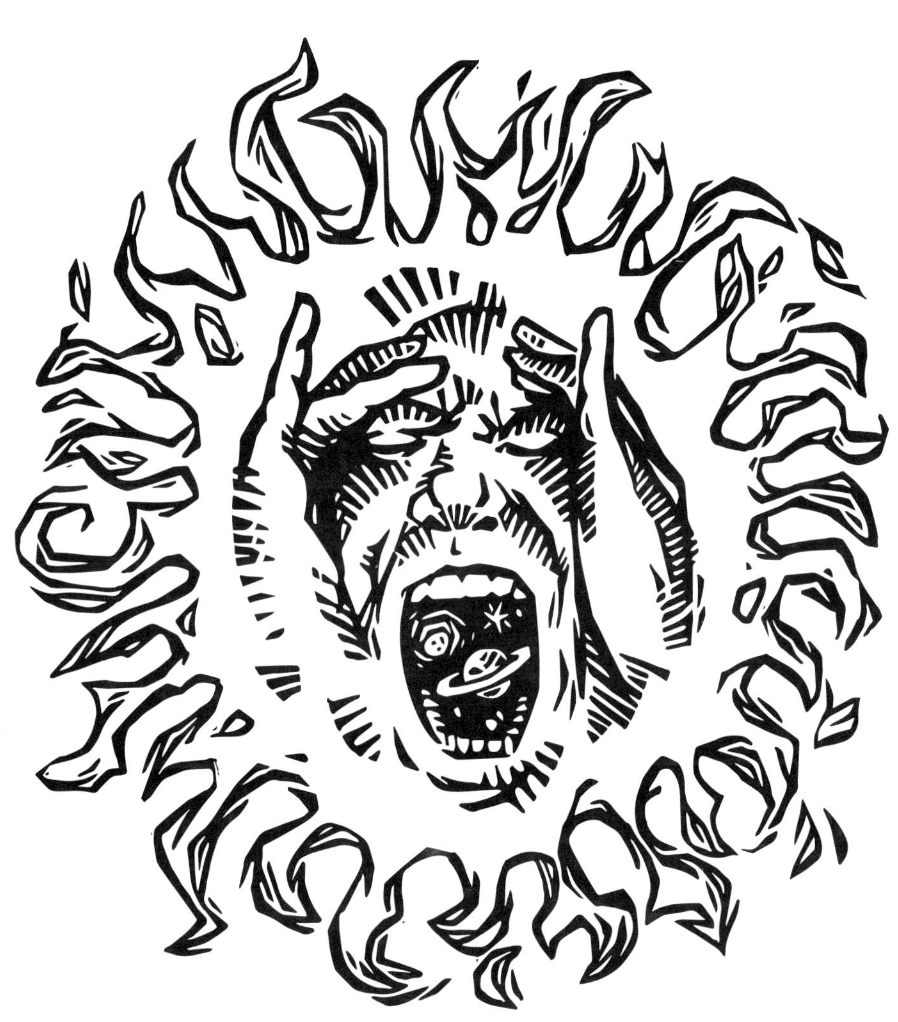

The Bigs

This is how the world starts. Not with a whimper but with a bang. According to the Big Bang theory, the universe began with an explosion of atoms and particles flung far and wide across the empty vacuum of space. Mighty chunks of molten dust like Earth settled long ago and now we're here, while the outskirts of the universe are still expanding. So what happens next?*

One possibility is the Big Crunch: Upon reaching the limit of expansion, contraction occurs and the universe abruptly snaps back into nothingness. Science suggests the expansion of the universe is speeding up, not slowing down, so this scenario seems unlikely.

Another theory is the Big Chill: Expansion continues until all particles in the universe get stretched too far apart. The loss of energy density creates a cooling effect, eventually becoming too cold to sustain life. The universe enters an extended period of emptiness.

The final theoretical response to the Big Bang is the Big Rip: The universe expands until it destabilizes and gets torn apart. This would split all matter, from large galaxies to subatomic particles, leaving an infinite space between everything.

Whether the universe pops like a balloon, shrivels like a raisin, or gets torn apart like an ex-lover's note, it's no urgent concern of ours. It will outlast our planet full of volcanos, floods, and disease. It will outlast our societies and their grave stories of certain demise. The universe will outlast us all.

---

* Besides the disproven theory of Indefinite Expansion, where everything is constant and the universe stays the same forever. But what's the fun in that?

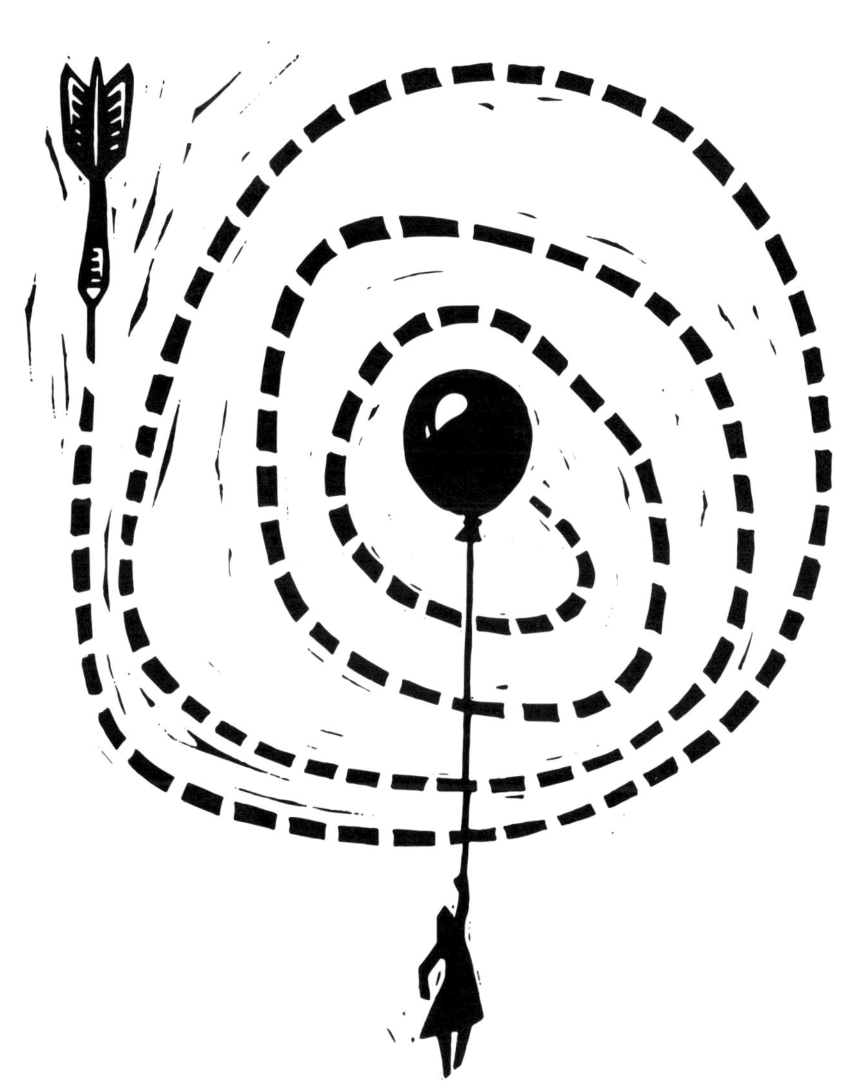

The End

The End is at hand. The tide rolls in, but this time into the streets of the old harbor town. The park you grew up in fills like a rusty sink. Murky sea rises while disappearing men quell sorrows. The newly emptied pubs are unburdened. Higher still, the water rises to the church on the hill that's been empty for even longer.

God has taken the day off. Bananas are brown. Animals have gone God-knows-where ages ago. Everyone has jumped ship—women and children, captain and crew, the scallywags, the sirens, the syphilitic, the rummies, the sinners and saints. For once, no one is around to send an SOS, so the vessel finds its own home.

The mountain has been carved to pave the road you took to leave town. Hot tar pours from the gashes, hissing as it touches the ocean. Across the still surface of the deepening water is the reflection of a cosmic rock that tears through the sky like it's cutting a perfect diamond. Wish you were here for the landing.

There's never enough notice to start over. Fixes were on sale but we waited too long and the deal expired. The lookout in the crow's nest gave up yelling into the neon sky. It used to be dark at night. Now there are shimmery nocturnal hotels, built but never filled, penthouse suites collecting dust on unworn carpets. Old books float by, given a burial at sea to their valuable lessons soon forgotten. The village elder was last seen reading news that hasn't been written. Whatever we're still mad about is water under the bridge, and water over it.

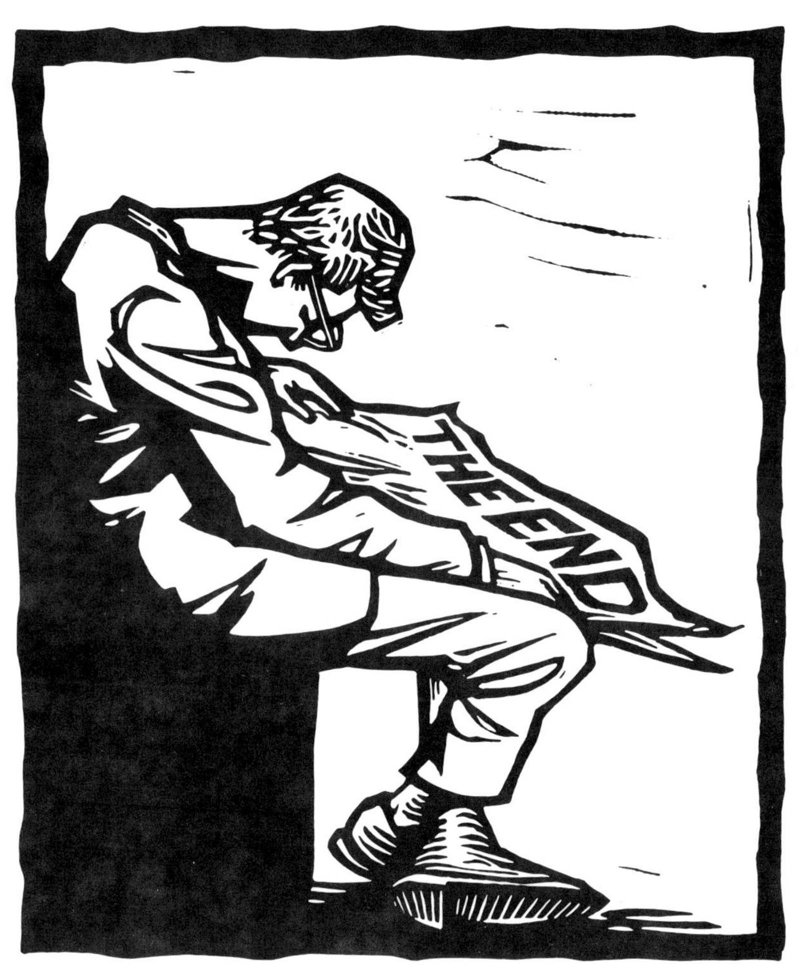
THE END

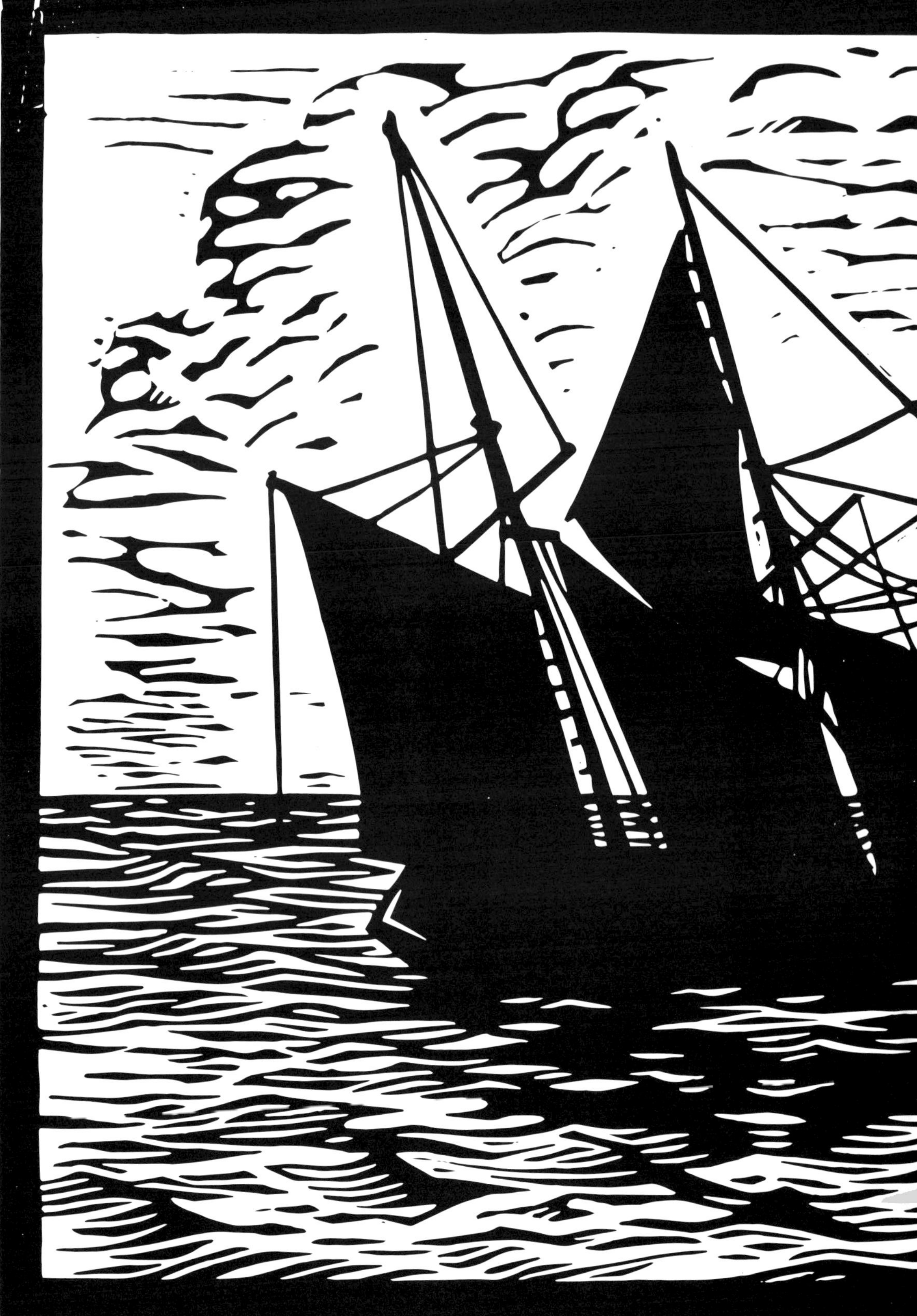

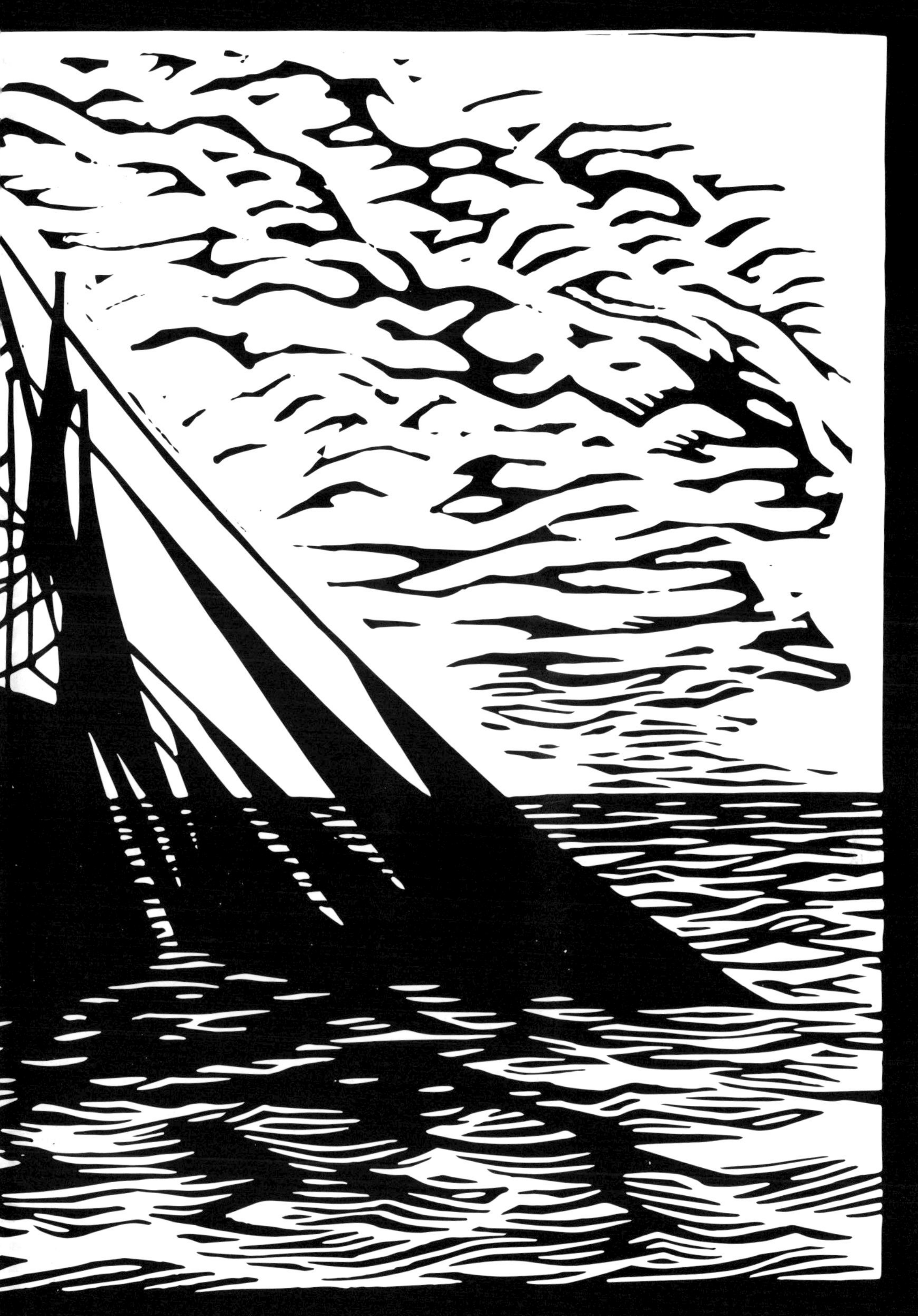

Bibliography

Mass Extinction

Bressan, D. (2016, February 1). "How Scientists Discovered The Extinction Of Species." *Forbes*. www.forbes.com/sites/davidbressan/2015/06/29/how-scientists-discovered-the-extinction-of-species

Greshko, M. (2021, February 10). "What Are Mass Extinctions, And What Causes Them?" *National Geographic*. www.nationalgeographic.com/science/article/mass-extinction

Volcanos

Fleming, N. (2015, December 18). "When a volcanic apocalypse nearly killed life on Earth." BBC. www.bbc.co.uk/earth/story/20151218-when-a-volcanic-apocalypse-nearly-killed-life-on-earth

Walsh, B. (2019, August 23). "A Giant Volcano Could End Human Life on Earth as We Know It." *The New York Times*. www.nytimes.com/2019/08/21/opinion/supervolcano-yellowstone.html

Astronomical Impact

Dorminey, B. (2017, February 2). "Earth And Moon May Be On Long-Term Collision Course." *Forbes*. www.forbes.com/sites/brucedorminey/2017/01/31/earth-and-moon-may-be-on-long-term-collision-course/?sh=5964fa4650d6

Greshko, M. (2021, February 10). "What Are Mass Extinctions, And What Causes Them?" *National Geographic*. www.nationalgeographic.com/science/article/mass-extinction

Eschatology

Landes, R. (2021, April 29). "Eschatology." *Encyclopedia Britannica*. www.britannica.com/topic/eschatology

Sameizade-Yazd, S. (2017, March 11). "How Religions Predict The World Will End." CNN. edition.cnn.com/2017/03/09/world/gallery/believer-end-of-world-prophecies/index.html

Noah's Ark

Conger, C. (2021, October 2). "Could Noah's ark really have happened?" HowStuff Works. history.howstuffworks.com/history-vs-myth/noahs-ark.htm

Kalki, the One Who Will End Time

"Kalki Avatar." (n.d.). Astroved Astropedia. www.astroved.com/astropedia/en/gods/kalki

Religious Conflict

Book of Revelation 12:7–10 New International Version.

"What does Revelation 12:7 mean?" (2022). BibleRef.Com. www.bibleref.com/Revelation/12/Revelation-12-7.html

Four Horsemen of the Apocalypse

"Four Horsemen of the Apocalypse." (2017, April 20). *New World Encyclopedia*. www.newworldencyclopedia.org/entry/Four_Horsemen_of_the_Apocalypse

Yajuj and Majuj

Quran Academy. (2017, June 19). "Yajuj and Majuj (Gog and Magog)." quranacademy.io/blog/yajuj-majuj-gog-magog/

The Editors of Encyclopaedia Britannica. (n.d.). "Yājūj and Mājūj | Islamic mythology." *Encyclopedia Britannica*. www.britannica.com/topic/Yajuj-and-Majuj

Extermination

Peck, R. (2021) *Exterminate All the Brutes* [Documentary Series]. HBO.

Ragnarök

McCoy, D. (2018, October 1). "Ragnarok." Norse Mythology. norse-mythology.org/tales/ragnarok/

Plague

Sullivan, A. (2020, July 21). "A Plague Is an Apocalypse. But It Can Bring a New World." *Intelligencer*. nymag.com/intelligencer/2020/07/coronavirus-pandemic-plagues-history.html

Namazu, the Earthshaker

Bressan, D. (2012, March 10). "Namazu the Earthshaker." *Scientific American*. blogs.scientificamerican.com/history-of-geology/namazu-the-earthshaker/

Cartwright, M. (2021, November 22). "Namazu." *World History Encyclopedia*. www.worldhistory.org/Namazu/

Stöffler's Flood

Strauss, M. (2009, November 12). "Ten Notable Apocalypses That (Obviously) Didn't Happen." *Smithsonian Magazine*. www.smithsonianmag.com/history/ten-notable-apocalypses-that-obviously-didnt-happen-9126331/

Doomsday Cults

BBC News. (2018, July 6). "Aum Shinrikyo: The Japanese cult behind the Tokyo Sarin attack." www.bbc.com/news/world-asia-35975069

Burton, T.I. (2018, April 19). "The Waco tragedy, explained." *Vox.* www.vox.com/2018/4/19/17246732/waco-tragedy-explained-david-koresh-mount-carmel-branch-davidian-cult-25-year-anniversary

Chiu, D. (2020, May 29). "Jonestown: 13 Things You Should Know About Cult Massacre." *Rolling Stone.* www.rollingstone.com/feature/jonestown-13-things-you-should-know-about-cult-massacre-121974/

Kaplan, D.E., & A. Marshall (1996, July 1). "The Cult at the End of the World." *Wired.* www.wired.com/1996/07/aum/

Parker, J.L. (2013, September 13). "Notorious Doomsday Prophets and Cults." CNBC. www.cnbc.com/2011/04/06/Notorious-Doomsday-Prophets-and-Cults.html

Rogers, K. (2021, March 26). "QAnon Has Become The Cult That Cries Wolf." FiveThirtyEight. fivethirtyeight.com/features/qanon-has-become-the-cult-that-cries-wolf/

Romano, A. (2019, August 7). "The Manson Family murders and Helter Skelter, explained." *Vox.* www.vox.com/2019/8/7/20695284/charles-manson-family-what-is-helter-skelter-explained

South African History Online. (2015). "A History of the Bulhoek Massacre." www.sahistory.org.za/article/history-bulhoek-massacre

Verhovek, S.H. (1998, March 4). "Taiwanese Group Prepares to Meet God -- in Texas." *The New York Times.* www.nytimes.com/1998/03/04/us/taiwanese-group-prepares-to-meet-god-in-texas.html

Locusts

Baskar, P. (2020, June 14). "Locusts Are A Plague Of Biblical Scope In 2020. Why? And . . . What Are They Exactly?" NPR. www.npr.org/sections/goatsandsoda/2020/06/14/876002404/locusts-are-a-plague-of-biblical-scope-in-2020-why-and-what-are-they-exactly

Rameswaram, S. (Host). (2021, April 9). "CICADAPOCALYPSE 2021." [Podcast]. *Today, Explained.* Vox Media. Transcript: docs.google.com/document/d/1qgG1TC1YRcaFNZkBWrJ8xyp7ln1yppkh-sEat9mQfF90

Zombies!

Ahmed, I. (2019, November 1). "The science of zombies: Will the undead rise?" Phys.Org. phys.org/news/2019-11-science-zombies-undead.html

Mariani, M. (2015, November 2). "From Haitian Slavery to The Walking Dead: The Forgotten History of the Zombie." *The Atlantic.* www.theatlantic.com/entertainment/archive/2015/10/how-america-erased-the-tragic-history-of-the-zombie/412264/

Walls, A. (2018, January 31). "The real public health science behind the zombie apocalypse." The University of British Columbia: School of Population and Public Health. www.spph.ubc.ca/26981-2/

Dark Day

Alfred, R. (2017, June 4). "May 19, 1780: Darkness at Noon Enshrouds New England." *Wired.* www.wired.com/2008/05/may-19-1780-darkness-at-noon-enshrouds-new-england/

The Prophet Hen of Leeds

Curzon, C. (2019, March 29). "The Terrible Crimes and False Wonders of Mary Bateman, the Witch of Yorkshire." *Mental Floss.* www.mentalfloss.com/article/577601/mary-bateman-witch-yorkshire-murder

Woman of the Apocalypse

Coates, S. (2019, August 23). "Delving Into The Mystery Of Joanna Southcott's Box." *Londonist.* londonist.com/2016/10/in-search-of-joanna-southcott-s-box

The Year Without Summer

Kohlstedt, K., & R. Mars (Hosts). (2021, September 10). "War, Famine, Pestilence, and Design." [Podcast]. *99% Invisible.* Radiotopia. 99percentinvisible.org/episode/war-famine-pestilence-and-design/

Steinberg, M. (2017, November 21). "The Year Without a Summer." *Old Farmer's Almanac.* www.almanac.com/extra/year-without-summer

Solar Storm

McFadden, C. (2020, May 30). "7 of the Strongest Solar Storms in Recorded History." Interesting Engineering. interestingengineering.com/7-of-the-strongest-solar-storms-in-recorded-history

Rosen, J. (2018, July 31). "Here's how the world could end — and what we can do about it." *Science | AAAS.* www.sciencemag.org/news/2016/07/here-s-how-world-could-end-and-what-we-can-do-about-it

Halley's Comet

Simon, M. (2018, July 19). "Fantastically Wrong: That Time People Thought a Comet Would Gas Us All to Death." *Wired*. www.wired.com/2015/01/fantastically-wrong-halleys-comet/

Chemical Warfare

Bressler, D.R., & C. Bakerlee (2018, December 6). "Superbugs and the risks of biotech: the next pandemic might be lab-grown." *Vox*. www.vox.com/future-perfect/2018/12/6/18127430/superbugs-biotech-pathogens-biorisk-pandemic

Nehme, J. (2018, April 9). "An effective killer: Five things you need to know about chemical weapons." International Committee of the Red Cross. www.icrc.org/en/document/effective-killer-five-things-you-need-know-about-chemical-weapons

Roos, D. (2021, May 17). "How the Shocking Use of Gas in World War I Led Nations to Ban It." *HISTORY*. www.history.com/news/world-war-i-gas-chemical-weapons

Alien Invasion

Schwartz, B.A. (2015, May 6). "The Infamous 'War of the Worlds' Radio Broadcast Was a Magnificent Fluke." *Smithsonian Magazine*. www.smithsonianmag.com/history/infamous-war-worlds-radio-broadcast-was-magnificent-fluke-180955180/

Temperton, J. (2021, April 20). "Neil deGrasse Tyson: We could all be pets in an elaborate alien zoo." *Wired* UK. www.wired.co.uk/article/neil-degrasse-tyson-intelligent-alien-life

The Sky is Falling

"Henny Penny." (2020, July 17). The Story Museum. www.storymuseum.org.uk/1001-stories/henny-penny

Schiefner, A. F. (2018). *Tibetan Tales, Derived From Indian Sources: Translated From the Tibetan of the Kah-Gyur* (Classic Reprint). Forgotten Books. www.pitt.edu/~dash/type2033.html#schiefner

Stump, T. (2016, December 30). "A Cartoon Takes on the Third Reich: Disney's Chicken Little (1943)." *Another Century*. anothercenturyblog.com/2016/12/30/a-cartoon-takes-on-the-third-reich-disneys-chicken-little-1943/

Nuclear Holocaust

Recchiuti, J.L. (n.d.). "The Atomic Bomb & The Manhattan Project." Khan Academy. www.khanacademy.org/humanities/us-history/rise-to-world-power/us-wwii/a/the-manhattan-project-and-the-atomic-bomb

Witze, A. (2020, March 16). "How a small nuclear war would transform the entire planet." *Nature*. www.nature.com/articles/d41586-020-00794-y

Doomsday Clock

Lerner, L. (2021, October 2). "The Doomsday Clock, explained." *University of Chicago News*. news.uchicago.edu/explainer/what-is-the-doomsday-clock

Hopi Mythology

Colavito, J. (2013, January 9). "Did the Hopi Predict the End of the World?" Jason Colavito. www.jasoncolavito.com/blog/did-the-hopi-predict-the-end-of-the-world

Kaiser, R. (1990). "Prophecies and Eschatological (Millennial) Traditions of the Hopi-Indians in Arizona." *Anthropos*, 85(1/3), 65-71. Retrieved from www.jstor.org/stable/40462115

McLeod, T. (2017, October 12). "A Hopi Messenger — Prophecy or Prediction?" *Sacred Land*. sacredland.org/hopi-messenger-prophecy-or-prediction/

The Cold War

Jitchotvisut, J. (2019, October 18). "What it was really like to live through the Cold War in America." *Insider*. www.insider.com/things-people-did-during-cold-war-bomb-shelter-duck-and-cover#children-learned-to-do-duck-and-cover-school-drills-1

Ward, A. (2018, December 26). "How a nuclear war kills you." *Vox*. www.vox.com/future-perfect/2018/10/19/17873822/nuclear-war-weapons-bombs-how-kill

Overpopulation

Abdelfatah, R., & R. Arablouei (Hosts). (2022, March 3). "Of Rats and Men." [Podcast]. *Throughline*. NPR. Transcript: www.npr.org/transcripts/1083527825

Piper, K. (2019, August 20). "We've worried about overpopulation for centuries. And we've always been wrong." *Vox*. www.vox.com/future-perfect/2019/8/20/20802413/overpopulation-demographic-transition-population-explained

Y2K

National Geographic Society. (2012, October 9). "Y2K bug." *National Geographic.* www.nationalgeographic.org/encyclopedia/Y2K-bug/

Murphy, C. (1998, November 23). "Y2K Computer Bug." *Washington Post.* www.washingtonpost.com/wp-srv/business/longterm/y2k/stories/consumer_faith.htm

Black Hole

Webb, R. (2021, March 24). "Has the Large Hadron Collider finally challenged the laws of physics?" *New Scientist.* www.newscientist.com/article/2272400-has-the-large-hadron-collider-finally-challenged-the-laws-of-physics/

Wild, F. (2018, August 22). "What Is a Black Hole?" NASA. www.nasa.gov/audience/forstudents/k-4/stories/nasa-knows/what-is-a-black-hole-k4.html

Mayan Calendar

National Geographic Society. "End of World in 2012? Maya 'Doomsday' Calendar Explained." (2011, December 21). *National Geographic.* www.nationalgeographic.com/science/article/111220-end-of-world-2012-maya-calendar-explained-ancient-science

"Why the World Didn't End." (2012, December 22). NASA. www.nasa.gov/topics/earth/features/2012.html

Global Warming

Brannen, P. (2018, March 22). "This is how your world could end." *The Guardian.* www.theguardian.com/environment/2017/sep/09/this-is-how-your-world-could-end-climate-change-global-warming

Vaughan, A. (2019, June 7). "Is it true climate change will cause the end of civilisation by 2050?" *New Scientist.* www.newscientist.com/article/2205741-is-it-true-climate-change-will-cause-the-end-of-civilisation-by-2050/

Solar Geoengineering

Mikulka, J. (2018, December 11). "3 Key Dangers of Solar Geoengineering and Why Some Critics Urge a Global Ban." EcoWatch. www.ecowatch.com/solar-geoengineering-risks-climate-change-2623070339.html

Artificial Intelligence

Swisher, K. (Host). (2020, September 28). "Opinion | Elon Musk: 'A.I. Doesn't Need to Hate Us to Destroy Us'" [Podcast]. *Sway. The New York Times.* www.nytimes.com/2020/09/28/opinion/sway-kara-swisher-elon-musk.html

Tegmark, M. (2018, April 1). "How to get empowered, not overpowered, by AI" [Video]. *TED Talks.* www.ted.com/talks/max_tegmark_how_to_get_empowered_not_overpowered_by_ai

Thomas, M. (2021, June 3). "The Future of AI: How Artificial Intelligence Will Change the World." Built In. builtin.com/artificial-intelligence/artificial-intelligence-future

Famine

Brändlin, A. (n.d.). "The Earth is Exhausted." *Deutsche Welle.* www.dw.com/en/the-earth-is-exhausted-were-using-up-its-resources-faster-than-it-can-provide/a-39924823

Cassella, C. (2019, October 7). "The World Could Soon Run Out of a Crucial Resource And Nobody Is Talking About It." *ScienceAlert.* www.sciencealert.com/the-world-could-soon-run-out-of-a-crucial-resource-and-very-little-is-being-done-about-it#

"Space Colonization." (2021, January 19). NASA. www.nasa.gov/centers/hq/library/find/bibliographies/space_colonization/

Sun Inflation

Carter, J. (2021, January 19). "This Is What We Will Look Like In 5.5 Billion Years When The Sun Is Dying." *Forbes.* www.forbes.com/sites/jamiecartereurope/2021/01/22/in-photos-this-is-what-we-will-look-like-in-55-billion-years-when-the-sun-is-dying/?sh=39a65c3d63c3

Loeb, A. (2019, November 25). "What Will We Do When the Sun Gets Too Hot for Earth's Survival?" *Scientific American.* blogs.scientificamerican.com/observations/what-will-we-do-when-the-sun-gets-too-hot-for-earths-survival/

The Bigs

"Fate of the Universe." (2015, June 29). NASA - Universe 101. map.gsfc.nasa.gov/universe/uni_fate.html

Siegel, E. (2018, June 30). "Ask Ethan: Could The Universe Be Torn Apart In A Big Rip?" *Forbes.* www.forbes.com/sites/startswithabang/2018/06/30/ask-ethan-could-the-universe-be-torn-apart-in-a-big-rip/

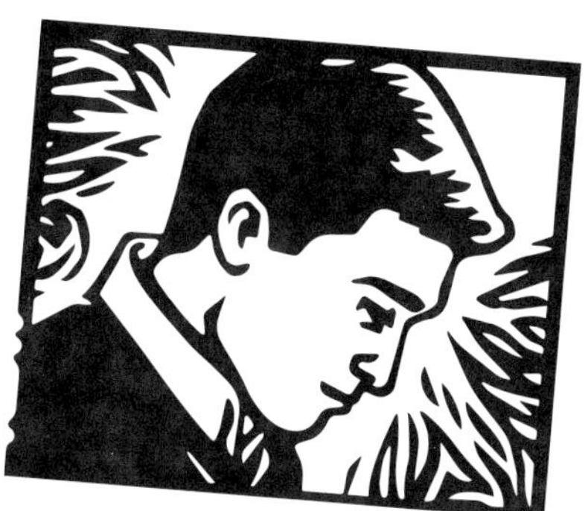

Darrel Perkins is an illustrator and printmaker from Providence, Rhode Island, USA. He currently lives in Dubai, UAE. The linocut illustrations featured here have been carved by hand, printed by press, then edited digitally. This book was made during the COVID-19 pandemic, one of many times in history when our world seemed to be nearing the end. Here's hoping for a good long life cycle.

exitus
adhuc
incertum

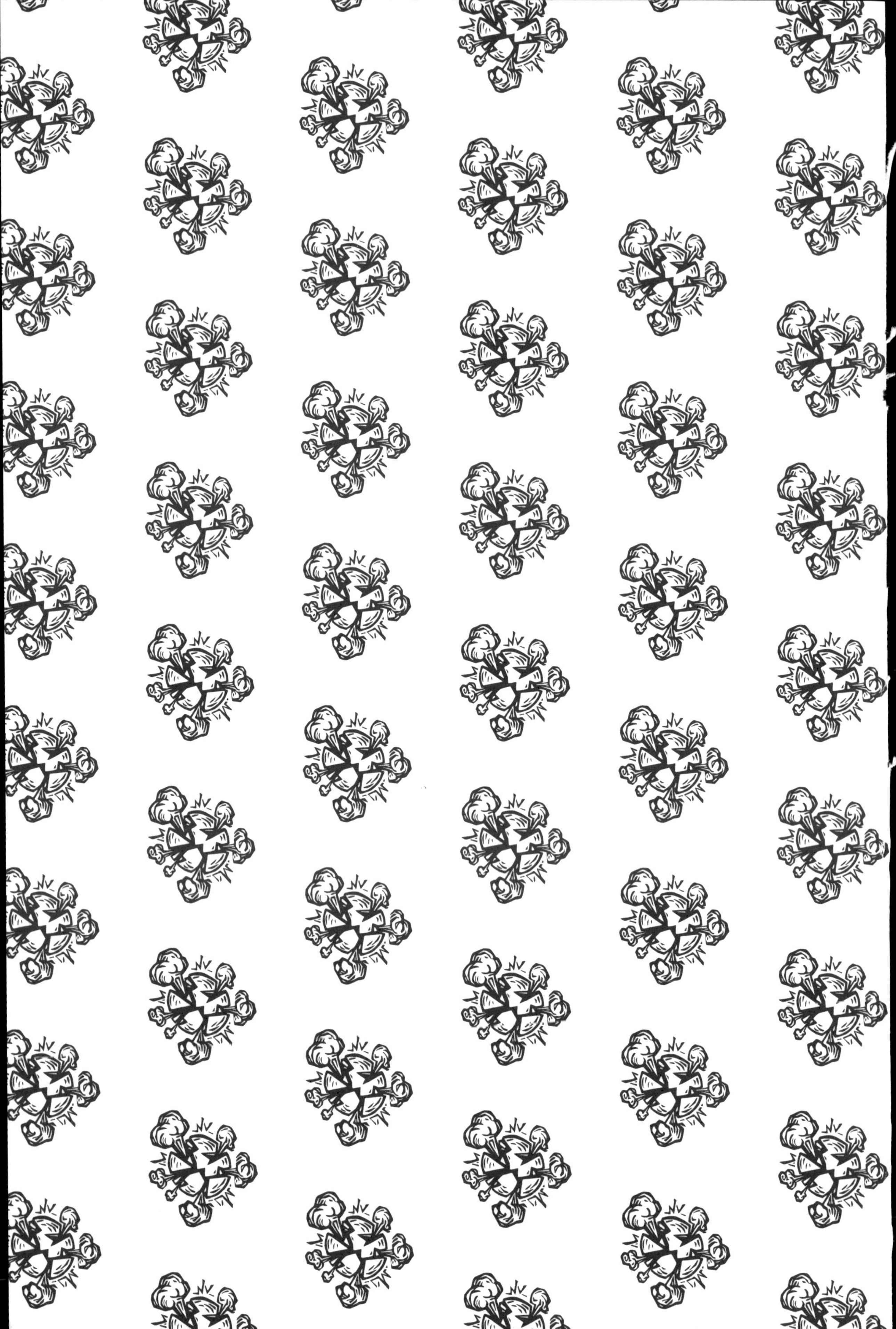